Doughnut Devotions

Doughnut Devotions

Humor-Filled and Inspiration-Glazed
Devotions for Your Spiritual Sweet Tooth

Lane McGullion

FaithTrek Publishing
Kennesaw, GA

FaithTrek Publishing
439 Two Iron Trail
Kennesaw, GA 30144
faithtrekpublishing@gmail.com

Special thanks to: Leon McIntosh and David Stuart for invaluable feedback. Tyler McIntosh for photography (see Unvld Photography on Facebook). Joanne Sher for editing (www.joannesher.com).

Visit my website at www.LaneMcGullion.com

First Printing: January 2014

ISBN 978-0-9913478-0-3

This book is dedicated to the following people

To my Savior, Jesus Christ – may the words of this book bring You the honor and glory that only You deserve.

To my parents – thank you for contributing more than DNA to my existence. Your love, guidance, and wisdom have made me the man I am today.

To my wife, Sonya – On Christmas Eve 1986, you flipped on a light switch and Chicago started playing in the background. After twenty-six years of marriage, you're still the meaning in my life. You're *my* inspiration.

To my children, Kayla, Cassidy, and Austin – being your dad has been a blast. There have been challenges along the way, but the joy has far outweighed the tough times. Your mom and I have done our best to show you Christ and encourage you to reach your full potential…so please pick out a good nursing home for us.

To our friends that have shared the journey with us – you have enriched our lives in innumerable ways. Fair warning – although names have been changed to protect the innocent, you may recognize yourself as a character in one of the enclosed devotions. If you're flattered to be included in a great piece of American literature destined to redefine the entire devotion genre, then yes, that's you. If you're offended, I was clearly referring to someone else.

Contents

Doughnut Devotions

The Saga of the Shopping Cart – The Theft

Sit back and hear the saga of the shopping cart – a tale of theft, intrigue, and revenge. The fable begins with the kindling of many similar anecdotes - three bored, teenage boys. In the sleepy, rural town of Sylvania, Alabama, the only real option for weekend festivities was to jump in the car and drive to the nearest metropolitan area (if you can call Fort Payne, Alabama "metropolitan"). A typical outing consisted of a movie followed by "cruising" around the McDonald's parking lot about a thousand times.

On a particularly boring excursion, we found ourselves at the local Kmart parking lot (for a change of scenery). That's when we saw the lone shopping cart at the end of the parking lot. The idea that would launch us into a life of crime was conceived.

"I wonder if that shopping cart would fit in your trunk," said my long-time friend who was a mischievous mastermind.

"Why?"

"Obviously, it's been abandoned. Let's take it."

"And do what with it?"

The three of us put our criminal minds to the task.

My other friend who had not really been engaged in the conversation piped up."Um, well, (thoughtful pause) we could take it over to Rhonda's house."

To the mind of a 17-year old boy, that made perfect sense. Certainly, an old shopping cart swiped from a parking lot would impress any teenage girl, right? It would prove once and for all that we were the "bad boys" that deserved her attention. Then maybe, just maybe, one of us would have a girl to cruise around McDonald's with. With the prize clearly defined, we put the well thought out plan into motion.

Have you ever tried to get a shopping cart into a car trunk while people are shouting for you to hurry? I don't know which took more damage, the cart or the trunk. We managed to almost get the trunk closed as we made our hasty getaway.

So, the obvious application here is "Thou shall not steal." However, what really set up the theft scenario was idleness. When people have nothing productive going on, they tend to find ways to get into trouble.

This is where I should point out the verse "Idle hands are the Devil's workshop." But, surprise, that's not in the Bible. Instead, we see the following sage advice: "Besides, they get into the habit of being idle and going about from house to house. And not only do they become idlers, but also busybodies who talk nonsense, saying things they ought not to" (1 Timothy 5:13) or in our case "taking shopping carts that don't belong to them." 1 Corinthians 15:58 reminds us to be "always abounding in the work of the Lord." Staying busy for Him will keep us out of a lot of trouble.

By the way, don't tell my mom about the shopping cart incident; she'll make me go apologize…30 years later.

Father, show us the importance of staying busy for you. Give us the energy and excitement for kingdom business. Keep us from the trap of idleness and laziness…and bored friends.

The Saga of the Shopping Cart – The Getaway

Let me set the scene – three newly minted criminals: the mastermind, the driver (me), and my third friend who is reading this now and still doesn't know what's going on, were now executing their getaway. The road back to Sylvania was a dark, curvy, mountain gap road. Adrenaline was coursing through our veins and I was looking in the rear view mirror for the police lights more than the road ahead of me.

Given all this drama, for some reason my buddy in the back seat thought it would be funny to reach his hand out and slap my driver's side window. I screamed like a girl. It took every ounce of skill to keep from driving off the side of the mountain. In hindsight, my hysterically laughing friend may not have been the best choice of cruising wingman.

When we arrived at Rhonda's house (on two wheels), we quickly unloaded our ill-gotten buggy. We knocked on the door and awaited the accolades.

"Hey, what are you guys up to?"

"Aw, nothing much," was the response, but we were really thinking, *You know, we're just a bunch of hooligans on the run from the fuzz.*

Puzzled, she asked, "Why do you have a shopping cart?"

"Oh, you noticed that?"

How could she not? My buddies were taking turns pushing each other up and down the driveway yelling "wahoo" at the top of their lungs. We were lucky there was nothing to build a ramp with. "Yeah, we swiped that from the Kmart parking lot."

"Okaaay…that's nice," she replied as she gave us the eye-roll that sealed our fate. "Thanks for stopping by, but I've really got to turn in. Early day tomorrow." And with that, the door slammed on our wooing-by-buggy-theft plan.

As we stood there with dazed looks, someone finally asked the obvious question, "So, what are we going to do with the shopping cart?" Seventeen-year-olds aren't really known for planning several steps ahead. So, we did what any person would do in that situation.

I can imagine the scene when her mom opened the door the next morning: pause, confused look, look around, scratch head.

"Rhonda, where did this shopping cart come from?"

We spend a great deal of time and energy trying to impress people, don't we? Don't get me wrong, it's important that we put our best foot forward and garner the respect of bosses, neighbors, friends, etc., but they're not the ones we should be trying to impress.

Paul knew this when he addressed the Galatians: "Am I now trying to win the approval of human beings, or of God? Or am I trying to please people? If I were still trying to please people, I would not be a servant of Christ" (Galatians 1:10). I doubt the Lord was very amused with our shopping cart antics.

Father, protect us from the misguided efforts to impress men. Show us the opportunities You give us daily to serve You and bring You glory. Lord, let us live lives that seek to impress You with our obedience.

The Saga of the Shopping Cart – Revenge

The shopping carts are out to get me! Call me crazy, but I'm convinced they have banded together for the purpose of avenging their fallen brother. I know, it sounds ridiculous, but the door dings on my car tell a different story. Let me give you one example.

Being a Southern boy, I have a fondness for barbecue in my DNA. At least once a week I'll venture over to my favorite barbecue place for lunch. I typically eat in my car under a shade tree located at the bottom of a hill in a nearby Target parking lot.

During a recent outing, I had just parked my new car and gone through the ritual food preparation. I was tuning in to my favorite radio program when I happened to glance up. The Target employee who had been rounding up a long row of shopping carts had somehow lost the front three.

The recently emancipated buggies were now barreling down the hill in a staggered attack formation that would have made the Blue Angels proud. After a quick trajectory calculation, I realized that they were on a collision course with my new car! So, barbecue was unceremoniously launched from my lap into the passenger seat and floor.

I started the engine and shot out of the way in the nick of time. I watched from my rear-view mirror as the carts went tumbling over the curb where my car once sat. From my open window I swear I heard an eerie whisper, "Next time, cart-stealer."

Unnerved, I eventually breathed a sigh of relief and proceeded to salvage what was left of my lunch. These days I park a few spaces over and keep a watchful eye for other kamikaze shopping carts bent on vengeance.

In what areas of your life are you making yourself a target? There is a solution: move. If you're tempted to pick up the wrong kind of magazine, avoid the magazine rack. If you have a problem with gambling, avoid the shining lights of Las Vegas. God has promised he will provide a way of escape when we are tempted (1 Corinthians 10:13). That "escape" can come through not putting ourselves in the crosshairs of temptation in the first place.

I also recommend a healthy respect for shopping carts. The shopping cart mafia is for real!

Father, help us see when we are making ourselves easy targets for the enemy. Give us wisdom to recognize our weak areas and strength to avoid situations where we may be compromised. Open our spiritual eyes and show us the ways of escape that you've provided in times of temptation.

White Noise for the Soul

Yawn.

I must yawn a hundred times a day. I'm a pretty light sleeper, so it's probably attributed to a lack of deep sleep. I seem to hear every little noise in the house after I lie down. A typical night goes something like this.

Drip, drip, drip.

We have a slow leak downstairs in the kitchen sink that I need to fix. Many a night I'll be lying in bed and my ears will hone in on it. I can't ignore it, so I tumble out of bed and downstairs to make it glance off the side of a dish or the sink wall.

Ah, that's better. Now to get some shuteye.

"Cough."

Which child was that? Maybe it was a one-time, clear-your-throat kind of cough. Just ignore it, maybe…

"Cough, cough."

I don't know many parents who can sleep if there's a sick child in the house; the parent Spidey-Sense won't allow it. Now where did I put that cough medicine?

Okay, she's better now, back to sleepy time.

"Woof."

Are you kidding me? Didn't I just walk you before I came up here? Or was that the neighbor's dog? Okay, make it quick. You're not living up to that "man's best friend" thing right now.

 OK, finally, I've got to get some sleep. C'mon Mr. Sandman, do your thing.

"Zzzzz-hghsmp-zzzZZZZ-ssffhgm-zzzzZZZ." (my best attempt at writing a snoring sound)

That's right – my lovely, sweet, and petite wife snores like Bigfoot learning to play a pipe organ. Oh, it's not every night, but sometimes…sheesh. After a few nudges, she finds the perfect angle for her nasal passages and all is well.

After a while I give up and resort to the only thing that seems to help – a fan on the highest setting. The "white noise" that it generates is soothing and drowns out all the competing noises for my ears's attention.

The other issue I deal with is simply turning my mind off. I will lie in bed and run through the day's activities, things I should have done, things I need to do tomorrow, how we are going to pay for those braces, what would I do if I won the lottery, wouldn't it be neat to be invisible…you know, important stuff like that. Mainly I dream up things to worry about – my job, the kids' future, home invasion scenarios, the evacuation plan if the house is on fire, etc. I need something like a fan to drown out those distracting thoughts.

Luckily, the scriptures give us some guidance: "In peace I will lie down and sleep, for you alone, Lord, make me dwell in safety" (Psalm 4:8). I've found if I can discipline myself to end my day with prayer and focus my thoughts on the Lord, it becomes "white noise" for my soul, drowning out the cares of the day. That is, until Bigfoot starts Act Two of Phantom of the Opera.

Father, we live in a world that offers us many distractions, distractions that cause us to take our eyes off You and lead to worry and despair. Lord, give us peace and rest. Keep our minds stayed on You and let us be rejuvenated to bring You glory.

Whoa is Me

I grew up in a rural area where horses were plentiful, but I never really had a desire to ride. However, when some friends offered to take us riding I thought, "Sure, why not?" We followed the typical trail ride technique, horses following each other at a leisurely pace.

After conquering that, I started channeling my inner cowboy so I asked, "Hey, can I take her out in the pasture and try a gallop?" My friend reluctantly agreed and soon I was at one end of the field giving my valiant steed a swift kick and a "Giddyup!"

The next few minutes are still a blur of terror and shouting "Whoa!" Judging from the start out the gates, my horse must have had some unfulfilled dream of competing in the Kentucky Derby. I had no control over that animal whatsoever. Soon, we were headed straight for a group of three cows minding their own business. I swear when they looked up I could see their eyes widen. Cows may look slow, but let me tell you, they can jump out of the way quickly when they see a screaming, colorless rider on an out of control horse bearing down on them.

After successfully dodging the bovines, I realized the tree line was rapidly approaching. Luckily, as I was calculating limb evasion techniques, my little filly decided it was time to stop...and head back across the pasture at the same clip. When we got back to our starting place, my friend just stepped in front of the horse and said, "Whoa, girl." I guess I had the wrong inflection in my voice when I said "Whoa" over a hundred times. No matter, I was just glad to find the ground on my own terms.

Needless to say, I'm not going to put a lot of trust in a horse in the near future, but that's not true of everyone. The psalmist writes that "some trust in chariots and some in horses, but we trust in the name of the Lord our God" (Psalm 20:7). Where do you put your trust? Your job? Your spouse? Your 401K? Your five-year supply of dehydrated food? I think we all see scenarios where trust in those things will fail us. But trusting in the Lord never fails. Walking with Him daily is the best security one can hope for. It won't always be easy, but neither is walking the day after an out-of-control horse ride.

Father, in You alone we place our trust. Friends and family may desert and betray us, but You never will. You are a faithful God who is closer than a brother. Thank You for the certainty that we can have in Your love.

Doughnut Bites

Doughnuts have been around for centuries, but most historians credit the Dutch with their invention in the mid-19th century. At that time they were known as olykoeks – "oily cakes".[1]

You're Not 17 Anymore

Getting older is for the birds. Lord willing, I have many years of life left, but things are certainly not what they used to be. I typically compare myself to the seventeen-year-old version of me, and the changes are becoming noticeable.

Seventeen-year-old Lane could run as many sprints as his basketball coach requested. Forty-seven-year-old Lane can't run 100 yards without his knees complaining, "Just what do you think you're doing?"

Seventeen-year-old Lane had a world of career opportunities to choose from. Forty-Seven-year-old Lane can't afford to start over in a new career with three kiddos to put through college. Seventeen-year-old Lane could stay up all night and be ready to go in the morning. Forty-Seven-year-old Lane has a long list of things to do after work, but following the long commute home he sits on the couch...and it's over. That list can wait another day. Forty-Seven-year-old Lane turns into a pumpkin at 10PM. Those are a few examples, but the list is much longer.

Aging also makes me think about my career coming to an end and what retirement might look like. I've been in the workforce for 26 years (47-year-old Lane had to resort to the calculator to come up with that number). I still enjoy my job as a project manager, but there are days when keeping up with other people's tasks, tracking project budgets, and reporting on status gets old. I can see a day when I'll be ready to walk away and try something new.

You'll notice I said "try something new." Many people think that retirement means playing golf or scrapbooking or traveling all the time, but that is contrary to God's plan. Work was always part of God's design for man.[2] We find fulfillment in an honest day's work and through work we relate to a God who is always at work in His creation.

You've probably heard someone say "there's no concept of retirement in the Bible." Well, that's not exactly accurate. There's no concept of ceasing from work, but there is precedent for stopping a specific job: "The Lord said to Moses, "This applies to the Levites: Men twenty-five years old or more shall come to take part in the work at the tent of meeting, but at the age of fifty, they must retire from their regular service and work no longer. They may assist their brothers in performing their duties at the tent of meeting, but they themselves must not do the work. This, then, is how you are to assign the responsibilities of the Levites" (Numbers 8:23-26).

You'll notice that at age 50, the Levites left active service and settled into more of a consultant role. I see that happening in my line of work as well. Seasoned project managers are able to move around from company to company sharing the skills they've acquired over the years.

The same should be true in the church. The heavy lifting is a job for the young. In this way we are actively training up the next generation of the church. But the older saints are not completely released from ministry to play golf all day. You'll notice that the retired Levites continued to serve as assistants. This allowed them to pass along the tricks of the trade and the wisdom acquired over their lifetime of service.

Seventeen-year-old Lane could probably write another devotion, but 47-year-old Lane needs a nap.

Father, make us eager to serve You and find the most appropriate ways to benefit Your kingdom. Let us not use youth or old age as an excuse for inaction. Give us a life-long desire to know You and make You know.

The Bonehead Episodes – Part One: Killer Carpet

Why is it that when you get injured, there's usually some bonehead explanation that has to be repeated over and over to your concerned friends? I mean, just once couldn't it go something like this:

"Oh wow, you're in a cast! What happened to your ankle?"

"Oh, this little thing? It's really nothing. I saw a guy getting mugged the other day and felt that it was my civic duty to help. As I was trying to break it up, the gun went off. I had just enough time to throw my ankle in front of the bullet. It's no big deal, but I thought the key to the city was a nice gesture."

When I tell the real story of how I broke my ankle, I can barely make eye contact:

"Oh wow, you're in a cast! What happened to your ankle?"

"It's kinda funny. I was sitting in Bible Study last Sunday morning. I had my legs crossed so I guess my foot fell asleep. I needed to run off to worship early, so I tried to make a quick, stealthy getaway, but my snoozing foot didn't get the message. I turned it over on a roll in the carpet. Smooth, huh?"

"So (insert suppressed chuckle here), you broke your ankle getting up from a chair?"

Yeah, no matter how I tried to spin it – boneheaded. Maybe I can salvage a little dignity by turning it into a spiritual application.

Paul warns us, "So be on your guard, not asleep like the others. Stay alert and be clearheaded" (1 Thess. 5:6, NLT). It's a crazy, fast-paced world out there and it's easy to get so wrapped up in "life" that you fall asleep spiritually. That's the opening the enemy is looking for. It may be something as simple as an angry response to a child or talking to that cute coworker a little too long. Be on the alert so you will be clearheaded, not boneheaded.

Father, keep us focused on You and spiritually alert. Wake us up when the enemy is on the prowl so we don't make a bonehead mistake that we'll have to explain over and over. And when we do trip and fall, thank You for Your grace, love, and forgiveness.

The Bonehead Episodes – Part Two: Killer Golf Balls

I like to play golf, but it's definitely a love/hate relationship. Ask anybody that plays and I imagine they'll tell you the same thing. Most of my rounds are a highlight reel for ESPN's "**Not** Top 10 List," but then there's that one shot; the shot that makes you say, "You know, I think I've about got this game figured out. With a little practice I could be on the PGA tour." After a dismal round, that one shot is the only one discussed in the clubhouse because "selective memory disease" is highly contagious on the golf course.

Unless, of course, there is an epic bad shot that your buddies just won't let go. Yes, I have one of those stories to tell.

Before I get to the details, you have to understand that I spend a lot of quality time with nature on the golf course since most of my first shots end up in the woods. Most golfers carry the traditional driver, irons, and putter in their golf bag. I also like to include a machete so I can get through the brush to my ball and a compass to find my way back to the fairway.

I was playing with a buddy one day and we both found ourselves in a wooded area. I had a good lie on a bed of pine straw and I could see the flag through the large pine tree trunks.

Most professional golfers would have realized that the best play was to chip the ball back out to the fairway to set up for a good third shot, but did I mention that the golf course is a breeding ground for boneheaded decisions? As I surveyed my options, I say to myself "Self, you can make that shot. You can put it right between those trees and on the green." Since I'm a pretty persuasive guy, I convinced myself to give it a go.

I grabbed my trusty five iron and coiled back like Casey for his final swing. I crushed that ball. As you may have guessed, my aim was a little off and the ball hit squarely in the center of a large pine tree only thirty feet away. I know it was dead center because the ball came right back in my direction with just as much force as I launched it.

From thirty feet and at that speed, there's zero reaction time. I'm still in my backswing when the ball returns to take its revenge. It nails me right in the side torso. Two inches higher and it would have cracked a rib; two inches lower and I would have needed hip replacement. I'm lucky I didn't rupture my spleen or something.

My golfing companion was a lifesaver in my moment of agonizing pain. His soothing laughter to the point of crying was just the salve that I needed for the circular, purple whelp that would be my companion for the next week.

What I could have used in that situation was a caddy. He would have talked some sense into me and hopefully persuaded me to take a wiser shot. He might have saved me from the recurring killer golf ball nightmare that plagues me to this day.

For the professional golfer, a trusted caddy is an invaluable resource. He knows the game back and forth. He knows the skill level of the player and can offer wisdom on how to play a shot. Sometimes he knows the golfer better than the golfer knows himself.

Similarly, we have access to the ultimate source of wisdom in our Heavenly Father. Don't get me wrong; I'm not suggesting we view the living God as our caddy; that would be irreverent. I'm saying that we should have that level of closeness and trust similar to that of a golfer and his caddy. Psalm 139:1-4 says, "You have searched me, Lord, and you know me. You know when I sit and when I rise; you perceive my thoughts from afar. You discern my going out and my lying down; you are familiar with all my ways. Before a word is on my tongue you, Lord, know it completely."

In hindsight, instead of asking myself or a caddy, I should have been addressing the One who knows me better than I know myself. He should be the one calling the shots.

Father, forgive us when we are headstrong and think we can handle life on our own terms. You are the giver of life and gave us the instruction manual in Your Word. Remind us to seek Your face daily for wisdom in our life decisions.

All the Cool Kingdoms Are Doing It

When my kids entered the teenage years, the boundary testing began in earnest. The clothes they wore, the movies they wanted to see, the music they listened to – everything seemed to be based on what their friends were doing. Friend envy, I guess.

I had to learn quickly how to explain why something they wanted wouldn't be good for them. For example, "Dad, why can't I go see Saw IV? Erin's mom is letting her go." My reply was well thought out and very Biblical – "Well, I guess Erin's mom doesn't love her as much as I love you."

OK, maybe that wasn't my finest hour. But, even though parents don't always get the words right, protecting our kids from what seems okay to other parents is an important part of child-rearing.

Israel faced a similar "nation envy" at the end of Samuel's reign as judge. They didn't like that they were different than the nations around them; they wanted a king to rule over them. God told Samuel to clearly explain to the people what having a king would mean – their sons drafted into the army, forced labor, and the "T" word (taxes). It fell on deaf ears.

1 Samuel 8:19-20 (NLT) says, "the people refused to listen to Samuel's warning. 'Even so, we still want a King,' they said. 'We want to be like the nations around us. Our king will judge us and lead us into battle.'" God, in his wisdom, gave the people what they wanted to prove that His word is truth. Eventually, the wicked kings destroyed Israel and the people were led into captivity.

Of course, we're much wiser than our children and the Israelites, right? Maybe not. Does the phrase "keeping up with the Jones" ring a bell? A wise man once said, "to compare is to despair." There's always someone a little smarter, a little better looking, or a better writer (hey, wait a minute). That's why contentment is a quality that we have to cultivate in our lives. God made us just how He planned and if we can't be content with that… I guess God loves us more than we love ourselves.

Father, teach us contentment. Keep our gaze fixed on You and not the neighbor's new car. It's just stuff anyway. The real prize is knowing You and growing closer to You every day.

Doughnut Bites

Elizabeth Gregory, a New England ship's captain, is the woman we have to thank for these tasty treats. She made them so her son could store a pastry for a long trip.

Careful, Your Motive is Showing

Parents, have you heard this one? "Dad, if I got a Smartphone I'd be able to use it for schoolwork and I could download a Bible app so I'd always be able to do my daily devotions." Translation – "Dad, I'd like to be able to text my friends 5000 times a day and there's a really cool zombie app that I want to download." A Smartphone might have the redeeming features mentioned above, but that wasn't the real motive behind the request.

I think we've all been guilty of a little rationalization, right? In fact, I thought I made a great case for a giant TV screen and surround sound in the basement. "Honey, the kids will have a great place to play the Xbox so we can have more alone time to cultivate our relationship." Translation – "College football starts in a month and I need a man cave so I can scream at the players without looking like a crazy man." The kids might get some Xbox time (during basketball season), but that wasn't the real motive.

Similarly, God is not fooled with our cleverness. In 1 Samuel 8:4-5, the elders of Israel approached Samuel and said, "Look, you're getting old and your sons are a couple of rascals. We'd really like to have a king instead" (my paraphrase). But the Lord knew the real motive. In verse 7, He states, "Listen to all that the people are saying to you; it is not you they have rejected, but they have rejected me as their king."

This wasn't a simple request to have a different man lead them. They didn't want to be under God's leadership any longer. Proverbs 16:2 (NLT) says, "People may be pure in their own eyes, but the Lord examines their motives." Did you catch that? We may even fool ourselves into believing the cover story, but the Lord knows us better than we know ourselves.

Father, teach to examine our motives. Show us where our desires are not aligned with Yours and then change our hearts. We love You and want to be men and women after Your own heart.

Doughnut Bites

Mrs. Gregory, concerned that the dough might not cook through, placed walnuts and hazelnuts in the center. Hence the term "dough nuts."

Let's Make a Deal

When I got my first job out of college, my wife and I made a startling discovery – we could buy stuff now! And buy stuff we did. We bought new furniture, new clothes, and a brand new, screaming yellow Geo Storm. Oh baby, that was a sweet ride.

Then we woke up from our spending binge (in our brand new waterbed) and realized we had accumulated a sizable amount of debt. Not wanting to be a "slave to the lender," we put our minds to work on how to clear up our debt quickly. That's when I had one of the worst ideas ever: I made a deal with God.

Oh, it seemed like a perfectly reasonable plan. We would suspend our tithing until we took care of the debt and then we would double up on the tithe until we caught back up. I figured the banks were charging me interest, so this was actually being a good steward, right? Right? Well, the financial wheels fell off our cart. We were literally inundated with unexpected expenses. It wasn't long before we got the message – it's not about the money, it's about obedience.

Malachi 3:8 asks a penetrating question – "Will a man rob God?" That passage makes it clear that the tithe belongs to God. Yes, the percentage is an Old Testament mandate, but for me and my house, 10% is the minimum starting place for giving that is commanded throughout scripture. Based on that conviction, to do anything other than gladly lay the tithe at His feet is to rob Him.

How arrogant of me to think that I could make a deal with God! Does the Lord need my money? Are the cosmic lights going to go out if God can't pay the light bill? Of course not. The point is honoring the Lord's command with our obedience. It took a financial whack on the side of the head, but we got the message.

We cleared up the debt at a slower pace, but it was a pace that honored the Lord through obedience.

Father, forgive us when our cleverness and selfishness get in the way of simple obedience. Give us a heart for being a part of Your plan instead of trying to force You into ours.

Doughnut Bites

Captain Gregory claims credit for giving the doughnut its signature hole, possibly by skewering it on a spoke on his ship's wheel when both hands were needed.

This One's for You

Obviously, this book is written to be an encouragement to those who follow Jesus Christ. However, it occurs to me that someone may read this book that doesn't understand the relationship that we have with Christ. In particular, a copy editor is going to edit my manuscript and graciously correct my grammatical errors, and they may not have any idea why Christ is so important to the rest of us. So this section is for you, my patient proofreader. The rest of you can take the dog for a walk or something.

So, why is Christ important? Because we have a problem that only He can solve.[3] You see, when God created us, He intended for us to have a close, loving relationship with him. But since the beginning, man has wanted to do things his way. The Bible calls that rebellion against God "sin" and every man is guilty.

The price tag for sin is high – physical death that culminates in spiritual death and eternal separation from God. The worst part is there's nothing we can do to fix this. No amount of "good living" or philanthropy can change our position with God. It's a death sentence. Pretty bleak, huh?

Fortunately, God wasn't done with us. He sent His only son, Jesus Christ, to live a sinless life and take our punishment. He didn't lift the death sentence; he transferred it to Jesus as He hung on the cross. When Christ rose from the grave, the Bible says He defeated death and made a path for us to join God the Father in heaven when we die.

In fact, he said it very clearly in John 14:6 – "I am the way, the truth and the life. No one comes to the Father except by me." The Bible says in Romans 10:9 that "if you declare with your mouth, 'Jesus is Lord,' and believe in your heart that God raised Him from the dead, you will be saved." It's a simple first step, but make no mistake, following Christ is not for the faint of heart. But no one who takes that first step has ever been disappointed.

Still skeptical, my trusty copy editor? Would it surprise you to know that the Bible predicts your skepticism? 1 Corinthians 1:18 (NLT) says, "The message of the cross is foolish to those who are headed for destruction! But we who are being saved know it is the very power of God." My prayer is that God will reveal Himself to you in a personal way, and that you might be able to reread this book someday through the eyes of faith.

Father, I pray for those that don't know the power of Your love. I pray that You'll reveal Your love to them and draw them into a saving relationship with Your son, Jesus.

The Scope of God - Bigger Than Big

"My dad is bigger than yours" is a common playground boast. Let's apply that challenge to our Heavenly Dad. How big is God? I'm not sure we can really grasp the extent of His creation, but let's give it the old college try.

Recently, the Voyager spacecraft left the solar system after a thirty-five-year journey. That's an astounding feat, but let's put it in perspective. Our solar system is one of many in the Milky Way galaxy. If the Milky Way were the size of a quarter, our solar system would amount to a speck of dust on the quarter. It takes a beam of light 100,000 years to cross it.[4]

Let's back it out again. The Milky Way is one of a countless sea of galaxies. Using the quarter as our scale, the next closest quarter-sized galaxy is over two football fields away. Scientists have taken pictures of the most distant observable part of the universe. It has taken light 14 billion years to get here from that point. Feeling small yet? Yeah, me too.

As scientists look farther out into the universe, we should be in complete awe that our God created it all. I get the idea behind the Big Bang theory, but at some point "something" came from "nothing." The only logical explanation for that is a creator.

Now try to wrap your mind around this – the majestic creator of the universe wants to have a relationship with us. Seriously? Psalm 8:3-4 says, "When I consider your heavens, the work of your fingers, the moon and the stars, which you have set in place, what is man that you are mindful of them, human beings that you care for them? " We are less than a grain of sand in the grand scheme of things, but according to the scriptures, He knows my name. He knows the number of hairs on my head.[5] It is simply more than I can process.

Father and creator of the universe, we are in awe of Your power and majesty. You are in all, above all, and beyond all. Help us to comprehend how great You are and how small we are. We praise You, mighty God.

Doughnut Bites

The doughnut really became a star during WWI when homesick soldiers were served the tasty treat as a reminder of home.

The Scope of God - Smaller than Small

The "crib sheet" is an effective mechanism for students seeking to get an advantage during a test. Unfortunately, it's cheating. I saw it all throughout high school - tiny notes written on notebook corners, soles of the shoes, palms of the hand, etc.

However, on occasion a professor would allow a single notecard with as much information as you could cram on it. It's amazing how much you can squeeze onto a 3"x5" space when a grade depends on it. Consider a strand of DNA – scientist have recently been able to store 700 terabytes of information on a single gram of DNA.[6] That's a pretty amazing crib sheet God created.

So, let's look at the other side of the universe for a moment. As difficult as it is to understand the expanse of the universe, it may be equally challenging to grasp how infinitely small our world is. As scientists continue to look farther out into the galaxy, they also look deeper into the smallest parts of the universe.

For many years, the only known subatomic particles were protons, neutrons and electrons. With advances in technologies we now see even smaller particles, such as quarks and bosons.[7]

The scientific community was all aflutter recently with the announcement that the elusive Higgs-Boson particle had finally been found. With this discovery scientists hope to prove why particles have mass.

Do you find it interesting that scientists have nicknamed the Higgs-Boson the "God Particle?" It seems that even scientists know they are reaching a stage in discovery that can only be explained by the existence of God.

The Bible speaks about God's role as Creator in John 1:3, which says, "Through him all things were made; without him nothing was made that has been made." Not only did He create, He is the glue that holds it all together. Colossians 1:17 (NLT) says, "He existed before anything else, and he holds all creation together."

We've explored the majesty of God at both ends of the spectrum – big and small. For a fascinating demonstration of this, I highly recommend the following website - www.scaleofuniverse.com.

Father, words are insufficient to express how amazing You are. Thank You for Your creation and for allowing us to catch even a glimpse of Your majesty.

Be Thankful

"Father we thank you for this day and your many blessings. We pray for your blessings on this food and our time together. In Jesus' name, amen."

Sounds like a perfect acceptable mealtime prayer, right? Maybe for the first thousand times, but after continuous repetitions, it starts to lose some punch…and probably some sincerity. Anything repeated over and over without any thought behind it can become meaningless. Consider the following example.

A friend of mine is an avid Auburn fan. In the fall he makes frequent trips to campus with his family to cheer on their favorite football team.

It's important for the story to note that there are no direct routes to Auburn without traversing some country backroads. Some of the homes on those roads are occupied by families who are struggling to get by, judging from the outward appearance.

One house in particular is little more than a shack on a barren field of dirt. When my friend passes by this house, he takes the opportunity to point out how thankful his family should be for what God has provided. But maybe, just maybe, he's made that point one too many times based on the following account of a recent trip.

"Hey, are you kids all right back there?" asks dad.

One of two sleepy heads rises up from the back seat, ""Yeah (yawn), where are we?"

After sleepily looking around for moment his son makes the realization, "Oh, never mind. We're at 'Be Thankful'," and lies back down before the familiar lecture begins.

There is no shortage of things to be thankful for – life, family, health, sight, employment, red velvet cake…and the list goes on ad infinitum. 1 Thessalonians 5:18 says, "give thanks in all circumstances; for this is God's will for you in Christ Jesus." I think most of us would whole-heartedly agree with this sentiment, but keeping it fresh and heart-felt is sometimes a challenge.

Father, the ways you bless us are beyond our comprehension, many we will never know this side of heaven. We're pretty good at thanking you for the big things, but help us to see the little blessings as well: a smile from a friend after a hard day, a fire on a cold winter night, and the kindness of a fellow commuter who allows us to merge into traffic. Please accept our thanksgivings offered with a heart of gratitude.

Beam Me Up, Scotty

One of the staples of science fiction is the transporter or teleportation device. If you need to get from place to place in space, it's awfully inconvenient to the story line to jump in a shuttle craft every time. That's where the transporter comes in. The transporter basically disassembles your body and reassembles it when it reaches its destination. It's a pretty handy tool to save the hero in the nick of time from an exploding planet or an alien attack.

Did you know there's recorded evidence of a successful human teleportation? In Acts chapter 8 we read an account where Philip was led by an angel of the Lord to an Ethiopian eunuch. Philip was able to explain the scriptures to the eunuch, which resulted in his salvation and baptism. After the baptism verses 39-40 say, "When they came up out of the water, the Spirit of the Lord suddenly took Philip away, and the eunuch did not see him again, but went on his way rejoicing. Philip, however, appeared at Azotus and traveled about, preaching the gospel in all the towns until he reached Caesarea." Suddenly took? Appeared? Sounds like a little Holy-Spirit teleportation to me.

Throughout history God has asked for volunteers to be His messenger. Isaiah 6:8 says, "Then I heard the voice of the Lord saying, 'Whom shall I send? And who will go for us?'" Isaiah had just witnessed a mere glimpse of His glory and eagerly answered back, "Here I am. Send me!"

For thousands of years, prophets and missionaries have taken the message of the Lord to every corner of the earth. These men and women of God have taken on a mission similar to Star Trek's exploring the final frontiers of space – to boldly go where no one has gone before.

How about you, my sister or brother;

Will you join the mission that is like no other?

To share his love wherever He calls;

To break sin's chains and formidable walls?

Like Philip of old to be whisked away,

Here am I, I'm ready! Send me, I say!

The Explosion Chronicles – Fun with Fireworks

A coworker recently told me about a trip he took to one of our rock quarries. He was expecting a run-of-the-mill trip to gather some requirements for a system upgrade, but that changed with one simple question:

"Wanna go watch us blow some stuff up?"

Uh, YEAH! You have to ask? Nothing taps into a man's inner teenager like "making things go BOOM!"

Flash back to the first time a guy sets off a firecracker. After the inaugural explosion, the next logical thought is "I wonder what would happen if I wired twelve of these things together and put it in my mom's flowerpot?" Exploding daisies, of course, followed by a lecture on the danger of fireworks from mom (and a stealthy "thumbs up" from dad).

Oh, the epic bottle rocket battles I had with my neighbor across the street. We created elaborate aiming devices to attempt to bring accuracy to our flaming projectiles (PVC pipe is best, for future reference). Did I mention he lived across the street? This added another skill dimension to avoid the occasional passer-by. There were more than a few close calls and last minute aborted shots when those vehicles came out of nowhere.

The more we battled, the easier it became to forget that we were dealing with some dangerous items. That "danger factor" was painfully brought to my attention on one fateful day. Bottle rockets were starting to lose interest so we upgraded to the next level. We started lighting individual firecrackers and throwing them at each other.

It was fairly easy to see a lit firework headed your way and sidestep out of the way. Unfortunately, I forgot about one I lit in my hand. While I was busy executing evasive maneuvers, it went off. "YEOW!" Searing pain ensued, but luckily, no lost digits. It's rumored that I broke the "men don't cry rule" on that fateful day, but those rumors are unconfirmed (sniff). I had a giant blood blister on my ring finger for days.

More importantly, I walked away from that incident with a healthy respect for fireworks. As kids, we often have a perspective that we're invincible. I think that's true of our spiritual life as well. That's why the Bible gives us a friendly reminder in 1 Corinthians 10:12 – "So, if you think you are standing firm, be careful that you don't fall!" I imagine we're all the same; there are areas in our lives that we "flirt" with sin, but we think we can dodge out of the way before it does any real harm. Be careful: there may be long lasting effects when that sin goes "BOOM!"

Father, give us wisdom to know when we're playing with fire. Show us those danger areas and give us the strength to put them down and apply that energy to Your Kingdom. Protect us, Father, when we're headed in the wrong direction and patch us up when things blow up in our faces.

The Explosion Chronicles – "Dannymite"

You wouldn't know it to look at him, but my dad was quite the football player back in the day. He played tailback and weighed in at a whopping 120 pounds, soaking wet. To avoid being crushed by an imposing linebacker, he had to rely on his secret weapon – speed. He was known for being able to explode through the line with a burst of speed and leave would be tacklers in the dust. That's how he got the nickname "dynamite" (or "dannymite," as he tells it) - a burst of power packed into a small package.

Dynamite is the mechanism that takes explosions from "fun" to serious stuff. And, believe it or not, it wasn't that long ago when dynamite was available for purchase at your local hardware store.

A friend of mine tells a tale about his dad buying some dynamite to help clear a field of tree stumps. His dad took him and another friend and taught them the process:

Step 1 – using an iron rod, poke a two-foot hole beside the stump

Step 2 – attach a long fuse and place a single stick of dynamite in the hole

Step 3 – light the fuse

Step 4 – run for cover

In a few moments a muffled "boom" would be heard with an accompanying small cloud of dirt. The stump would be uprooted enough to make clearing a simple task. Dynamite made the process much easier than digging the stump out.

After watching dad work the process for a few stumps, he let the boys do the hands-on work until he was confident they understood the process. Then, in what contemporary parents would consider horrifying, he left them to clear the rest of the field. Sixteen year old boys + dynamite = trouble waiting to happen.

The first couple of stumps went as expected. Everything to this point had been average sized stumps, less than a foot in diameter. However, the recently crowned demolition experts soon faced an unexpected task: a stump that was four feet wide.

After making what seemed like a logical calculation, the boys decided that eleven sticks wired together would be needed to uproot the vestige of the giant oak. The holes were prepared, the sticks placed, and the fuse prepared. When the fuse was lit, the boys hightailed it about fifty yards to the tree line and awaited the results with racing hearts. Time seemed to stand still.

"Maybe we should go…"

"KA-BOOOM!" As my friend tells it, the earth literally shook with the force of the explosion. The stump, which seemed an immovable object, had now become a projectile. It sailed in their direction, over their heads, and landed in the woods about fifty yards behind them. After a few moments to process what just happened, the obvious was stated. "Do NOT tell my dad about this!"

Clearly, the boys with the dynamite didn't fully realize the power they had at their disposal. I wonder if we have a clear picture of the power we have at our disposal in Christ? Ephesians 3:20 says, "Now to him who is able to do immeasurably more than all we ask or imagine, according to his power that is at work within us." Christ's power, the power that created the universe, is at work in us! Talk about a secret weapon!

So, when the linebackers of failure, despair, and hopelessness look like they are going to mow you down, unleash a little unexpected power.[8] Light the fuse of prayer and run for cover under His sheltering wing. Then wait for the "KA-BOOOM!"

Father, help us realize the power that we have at our disposal. Your Holy Spirit dwells in us and gives us the ability to stand against any enemy and any fear. Remind us to turn to You in those moments when the obstacles seem insurmountable. Lord, thank You for spiritual "dannymite!"

The Explosion Chronicles – The Shockwave of Golgotha

I know what you're saying. "Lane, what about blowing up stuff at the rock quarry?"

Sorry to leave you hanging like that. So, my coworker headed out with the site crew to view what he believed would be an impressive display of explosives. However, when they got to the viewing area, he found out they were still about 300 yards from the blast site. The blast area was about 2 inches high from that distance. Needless to say, expectations dropped considerably.

Donned with the appropriate safety gear, they awaited the fireworks. As expected, when the blast was set off the visual display from that distance was a small puff of dust (insert half-hearted "Hurray" here).

Then the shockwave arrived. "BOOM!" It caused my coworker to literally take a step back due to the force of the blast. He said one of the ladies that accompanied them gave a little shriek. Unexpected would be an understatement. One of the site crew said he felt safe that they were outside the radius of falling rock – at 300 yards!?!? Wow, that's some power!

We've all seen videos of the ultimate display of man's destructive power: the blast wave of an atomic bomb. A fraction of a second after a nuclear explosion, the heat from the fireball causes a high-pressure wave to develop and move outward, producing the blast effect. The front of the blast wave travels rapidly away from the fireball, creating a moving wall of highly compressed air resulting in significant destruction.[9]

I would submit that what Christ did on the cross produced an even greater shockwave that continues to this day. Return with me to Golgotha – the Savior hangs on a cross, beaten so badly the Bible says He no longer looked like a man.[10] All the sins of man - past, present, and future - are heaped onto His back until the task was completed and He spoke His final words.

"It is finished!" And with that, the explosion of redemption was detonated. There was probably silence at Calvary in that moment, but in the spiritual realm – "KA-BOOM!"

- Immediately, the veil in the Holy of Holies was torn from top to bottom

- Three days later, Christ burst forth from the tomb. In conjunction with His resurrection, many Old Testament saints were observed risen from the dead as well.[11]

- The shockwave continued with the gift of the Holy Spirit at Pentecost. With that jolt of power, His disciples began the expansion of the gospel to the uttermost parts of the world.

The shockwave continues today. As we share the truth with those around us, chains are broken, hearts are mended, families are restored, and souls are saved. So, put on your hardhats (i.e. the helmet of salvation), because there's still work to be done. It can get messy, so watch for debris.

Father, it's hard for us to grasp the scope of what occurred on Calvary, but we witness the results even today. Give us a burden to be an active part of the "demolition team;" tearing down the enemy's strongholds and bringing the Gospel to those who need to hear it.

The Stranger

I was nudged from a Sunday afternoon nap by my smiling six-year old daughter.

"Daddy, there's somebody at the door."

About two more seconds of partial sleepiness passed before I realized what that meant. Cue the adrenaline. I proceeded to jump from the bed, stub my toe, and rumble down the stairs to find the front door standing wide open with a smiling door-to-door salesman patiently waiting to sell me his wares. Clearly, it was time to have the "don't open the door to strangers" talk with my daughter.

The art of "when to open the door" is a crucial suburban survival skill. Newspaper salesman, college kids with coupon books, Jehovah Witnesses – there seems to be no end to the people at the door who want something.

However, the biggest threat to my wallet (and waistline) is the Girl Scout Cookie Commandos. It's imperative that we present a unified front as a family or we will surely be drowning in Samoas. Resistance is futile when those pleading eyes make contact.

Joking aside, it's a cause for concern when our kids start opening the door for people they don't know. So, it was time to teach that important lesson to my six-year old daughter. Knowing that words don't always make the point at this age, I decided to be clever and do some role playing to illustrate. I told my daughter that I was going to pretend to be "the stranger" and that I was going to knock on the door. She was supposed to say "Who is it?" When I didn't answer, she was supposed to go get mom. Sounds simple, right?

Knock. Knock.

My daughter opened the door (sigh). Okay, let's try this again. After re-explaining the scenario, my daughter assured me that she understood and we reset the stage for our little drama.

Knock. Knock.

My daughter simply opened the door again. Color me flabbergasted. That's when I decide to improvise and go off-script to hopefully make my point. I grabbed my daughter and started running out the door and across the yard. My impromptu abduction worked a little too well; my daughter was genuinely frightened by the whole ordeal. Later that night I was listening outside my daughter's room as my wife was tucking her in.

"Daddy's not going to play the stranger anymore, is he?" she said with the slightest of quiver in her voice.

Sonya assured her that she was safe and that I was just going to be "Dad" from now on. I felt bad for frightening her, but I did make my point. The door wasn't opened for strangers any more. I have noticed, however, that I'm running a little low on Thin Mints.

It's human nature to be wary of "the stranger" - someone who is out of place, who doesn't belong. Do you know that as a follower of Christ, YOU are the stranger? 1 Peter 2:11 (NASB) says, "Beloved, I urge you as aliens and strangers to abstain from fleshly lusts which wage war against the soul." We are strangers in this world; our real home is Heaven. We should not be surprised when people give us a wary look - we're different!

Do you know how not to be a stranger anymore? Introduce yourself. Strike up a conversation that maybe leads to a friendship. Over time, the Lord may give you the opportunity to explain why you're "different." If they choose to follow Christ, then you will make a stunning metamorphosis from stranger to brother or sister.

Father, help us to look different from the world by looking more and more like Christ. At the same time, give us the desire to find opportunities to explain why we're different.

Doughnut Bites

The first doughnut machine was introduced in 1920 by Adolf Levitt in New York City. I wonder if he had a hot light too?

Send Me an Angel

God answers prayers. For me, those answers have not generally been accompanied with a "burning bush" experience where God is physically present, but I can clearly see the answers in other ways, such as a peace in my spirit or confirmation from a brother or sister. There was one time, however, when I was blessed to have an answer delivered by angels. No, really. Well, kinda.

My wife and I had been struggling for several months over the choice of schools for our oldest daughter, Kayla. She had a really tough time the last couple of years in elementary school and the "ladies" that made her life miserable in elementary would be waiting for her in middle school. Too many tears were shed those years; we needed to act. So, we began to pray for direction.

There aren't a plethora of options available to the parent when it comes to schooling. We prayerfully considered the following:

1. Continue at the middle school we're zoned for and see how it goes – I don't want our children to ever shy away from a situation just because it's hard. And I don't think the next generation has much hope if all the Christian kids pull out of public schools. Being actively engaged with the world is an ideal I believe in, but we needed to determine if our child was up for the challenge.

2. Move to another district – yes, we could move, but there's no guarantee that the kids at the new school would treat her any differently. For those that haven't raised a child through middle school, I firmly believe it's the hardest years of school from kindergarten to PhD. The academic

expectations are quickly accelerated, but that pales in comparison to the social acceleration. Middle school kids are exposed to every adult concept via TV and the internet, but haven't matured emotionally to be able to handle them. It creates a rush to adulthood and a wide chasm of maturity for those that want (and need) to be a kid a little longer. So, public school in general didn't give us a warm and fuzzy feeling.

3. Homeschooling – my wife has a teaching degree, so, on the surface, homeschooling would seem to make sense. However, knowing my wife's and my child's personalities, that would have been asking for World War Three. I'm sure there would have been moving ballads written about the "Battle of Algebra Hill," but it just wasn't worth the harmony of the home that would be lost.

4. Private school – there were a couple of good Christian schools in the area. The idea of a Christian environment was obviously appealing, but the price tag was not. We would have to make some sacrifices to make this option work.

5. Truancy – Seemed like a good option until l learned I could go to the pokey. I don't look good in orange.

So, there were several options on the table. We prayed for several weeks and didn't get a clear direction. Frankly, I was starting to get a little frustrated with God for not giving us…something…anything. Time was growing short and we needed an answer! At the pinnacle of my angst, I took half a day off and went to a park by a local river. I wasn't going to leave until God gave me an answer! I know, trying to force God's hand is not the best game plan, but God was gracious to a frustrated father that day.

I prayed earnestly over the options and listened intently for a reply. Over time, the Lord allowed me to sense a peace about the private school route. I was overjoyed to have an answer. I praised the Lord for giving me clarity.

That's when angels showed up to confirm what the Lord had revealed. No joke. As soon as I said "Amen," the Blue Angels screamed over the top of the treetops in perfect formation. It was deafening. They were in town practicing for an airshow, but I truly believe they were there for another reason: to graciously confirm a father's prayer.

Father, thank You for the promise in Proverbs 15:29 that You hear our prayers. Give us patience when the answer requires us to wait, sometimes for long periods of time. Comfort us in those times when You are silent and bolster our faith until You graciously lead us to Your heart.

Telemarketers, Salesmen, and Mormons – Oh My!

Now that everyone in my family has a cell phone, we get very few calls on our home phone. When it does ring, there's a high likelihood of a telemarketer on the other end of the line who wants my money. Or my time to do a survey. Or my old clothes for charity. You get the idea - everybody seems to want something.

How I handle these calls is really determined by what kind of mood I'm in. Sometimes I let them go through their whole spiel and politely say "no," but typically the call goes something like this:

"Hello?"

(pause before coming on the line) "Hello, is Mr. (butchered pronunciation of my last name) there?"

Click.

Yes, I just hang up. My children think that is very rude, but telemarketers know the score, right? In my mind, I'm doing them a favor so they can move on down the list to the their next victim (I mean, potential sale). At least I've changed my method from when my kids were younger. I'd tell the telemarketer, "You should talk to the decision maker in our house" and hand the phone to my five-year old. Those conversations didn't last very long.

I think if we're honest, we tend to view telemarketers as modern day lepers. We'd really prefer that the caller ID would just say "UNCLEAN" so we could ignore the call. C'mon, you know it's true.

Unfortunately, that association is sometimes deserved. We had a credit card stolen a while back which eventually caused some charges to get sent to a collection agency. I tried to explain the situation when the collector called, but they just proceeded to talk ugly to me. What could have been handled with civility was unnecessarily confrontational.

On another occasion, my wife got over fifty calls from several different telemarketers over the course of three days looking for "William." They desperately wanted to lend him some money. We thought we were going to have to change her number, but they finally stopped.

Similarly, I've never met a door-to-door salesmen that was just dropping by to say "Hi." The face-to-face sales pitch is even worse, because I can't bring myself to close the door in someone's face. So, if I look through the peephole and see a clipboard, that doorbell is going unanswered.

I'm also not going to open the door if there are a couple of guys in white shirts and black ties standing there. You'd think they'd come up with a better disguise because they are a dead giveaway. When I spot them in the neighborhood on my way home, I burst through the door and say "Nobody open the door, there be Mormons out there!"

Whenever I avoid people who are trying to sell me something - a new phone plan, a vacuum cleaner, or their religion - I feel a twinge of guilt. Why? Because, as a Christ-follower, I should be treated that way every day.

Telemarketers and their ilk have a message they are trying to communicate with the hope that we will see the value of what they have to offer. Likewise, we have the most important message that has ever been entrusted to a people to deliver...the Gospel.

Christ said in Luke 6:22, "Blessed are you when men hate you, when they exclude you and insult you and reject your name as evil, because of the Son of Man." If you and I are regularly communicating the message of the Gospel, we will be insulted, rejected and avoided with as much gusto as a telemarketer.

Kinda puts the telemarketer in a little different light, huh? Maybe a bit of a kindred spirit? So, here's a challenge for you and me - the next time we get that call, offer to listen to their message if they'll listen to yours. It just might result in an eternal transaction.

Father, forgive us when we avoid people because we don't want to be bothered. Forgive us when we avoid our mission to share the Gospel. Help us to embrace being avoided and rejected for Your sake instead of fleeing from it. Our window of time on this earth is short; help us to complete our mission.

All Aboard! The Humility Train is Leaving the Station

I've never been much of a "Hey, look at what I did" kind of guy. I usually let my actions speak for themselves without feeling the need to call people's attention to them. I enjoy the occasional public accolade, but at the same time it makes me a little uncomfortable.

There was one time, however, much to my chagrin, that I totally jumped off the humility train for some egregious showboating.

Our pastor preached a sermon on being plugged in and involved in the ministry of the church. His point was that we overload those that are willing to serve with too many things when we should be able to spread the work of the Kingdom across the entire body.

To prove his point, he asked everyone to stand up who was involved in a ministry of some kind at the church. Then he asked everyone to remain standing if they were involved in two ministries. I could see where this was headed and started doing the math in my head. I remained standing with those involved with three ministries. After I sat down, I remember three additional ministries that I was involved in. I'm thinking, "Wait a second, let's start over, I have more ministries!"

That's when the humility train pulled away from the station and left me at the self-righteous depot. I came back for the second service and planted myself in the front row, baby! Everyone was going to see that I was super-Christian guy involved in a whopping six ministries.

After my moment in the sun, I sat back down. That's when I clearly heard the Holy Spirit say, "So, are you feeling pretty good about yourself?" My moment *in* the sun was about to turn into a moment *with* the Son.

I was reminded that all of our righteous acts are like filthy rags[12] in comparison to His glory and majesty. I was literally trying to grab some glory for myself that He alone deserves. I went from standing tall and proud to feeling about two feet tall and wanting to slink out of the sanctuary. Learning my lesson, I put my hobo clothes back on and jumped in an empty boxcar of the humility train for some serious knee-time.

Father, forgive when we strut around and think we're pretty hot stuff,

Remind us of Your glory and our service is never enough.

Teach us true humility and forgive us of our pride,

Return us to the primary Vine in which we shall abide.[13]

You'll Never Catch Me Alive Copper!

I haven't received a traffic citation in a long time. I think I'm starting to drive like a grandpa a little before my time. However, back in the day, I was a little too heavy on the pedal. I received my first citation when I was 16 and I felt it was completely justified. I was driving on a two-lane road behind a Trans Am doing 40 in a 55.

"C'mon, you're a Trans Am, for crying out loud! You should be ashamed of yourself."

This driver deserved to be passed simply for underutilizing his ride. So, I hit the turbo booster in my Oldsmobile Omega (i.e. turned off the AC) and flew around this Smokey and the Bandit wannabe. Unfortunately it was on a double-yellow line. The long arm of the law was more than happy to educate me on the finer points of traffic safety.

Admittedly, that fell squarely in the stupid category, but that pales in comparison to one of my finer moments. I was on my way to the thriving metropolis of Fort Payne, AL, when I hopped on the interstate for a quick jump over to the next exit. I came off the onramp building speed like Evil Knievel approaching seventeen buses. About that time I noticed the police car approaching on the opposite side of the freeway. I'm doing at least 75, but I swear our eyes met. He's clearly got me dead to rights. Of course, the logical thing to do would be to slow down and hope he's got better things to do. Did I mention I was seventeen? Logic and seventeen year olds rarely cross paths.

"If I can just get to the next exit, I can lose him!"

I don't know if it was the James Bond marathon or what, but before I know it, I'm accelerating to try and lose the cop. I can see in my rear view mirror that the police car is turning around in the median. I'm probably approaching 90 miles an hour when reality finally breaks through.

"You idiot, you're trying to evade a police officer. You are going to jail."

I pulled my car over and waited, hoping he missed that whole acceleration thing.

"Is there a problem, officer?" I'm sure I was as pale as a ghost.

"Well, son, I was gonna let you slide, but I saw in my mirror that you sped up and passed another car. License please."

Luckily my life of crime was cut short by coming to my senses.

I don't know about you, but it's comforting to me to read the Bible and see that the people God used in a mighty way also struggled with lapses of rational thinking. Take Jonah, for example. In the first chapter we see God give Jonah a command to go the city of Ninevah and preach. Not being a big fan of the Ninevites, Jonah accelerates and tries to outrun the Lord. He catches the first ship out of town.

"If I can just make it to Tarshish, I can lose him."

Well, we all know how that worked out. Instead of issuing Jonah a citation, God put Jonah in fish jail for a few days before sending him on to complete his task.

Jonah's story makes me wonder - how much pain and suffering do we inflict on ourselves by not simply complying with the Lord's initial request? He's never going to ask for more than we can handle and he'll strengthen us for the task.

Unfortunately, we often let fear or anger or past failures get in the way of timely obedience. If you're struggling with something that you feel the Lord wants you to do, take a minute and pray - you might have just have a moment of clarity of your own.

Father, give us courage to follow You, even when it scares us to death. We know You are faithful and will not ask beyond what we are capable. Give us clarity Lord, and strength to be obedient.

The World is Moving On

"Be home by dark."

When I was growing up, that was about all the interaction I had with my parents on some Saturdays. I would head out on my bike with one of my friends and we'd be gone. If my parents needed to find me…good luck. I rode every dirt road and pig trail in the county until the sun went down.

The best thing was - I never felt like I had to worry about being safe. No one was ever abducted. No one ever disappeared. It was a simpler time.

Not so today; I have to know where my kids are every second of the day. When they ride their bikes, they are allowed to go from a designated mailbox to another, all within line of sight of the house. Am I overprotective? Maybe, but I also think the world has moved on.

Think about high school. Where I grew up, people could pray at events without fear of being sued. Pastors were welcome. There might have been a couple of kids that smoked, but drugs were rare (or very well hidden). Kids may have goofed off and gotten into trouble, but there was a healthy respect for teachers. None of that seems to apply today. The world has moved on.

Take the comparison to the national level. I wasn't all that in tune with politics back then, but it seems the political parties weren't so diametrically opposed. There was effort to cross the aisle to get things done. The issues were more focused on economics and foreign policy. Now it all seems to be about retaining power. There's no middle ground anymore – you pick a party and defend the platform whether it makes sense or not. More and more issues are social in nature and judicial rulings are slowly stripping away the Christian principles that undergirded this country from its infancy. Yes, the world has moved on.

As the world barrels down its progressive road, I wonder if it ever looks in the rear view mirror. Most companies have learned to do self-evaluations to determine if they took a wrong turn. The successful companies will have the courage to say, "Well, that was a mistake" and take a different course.

Remember New Coke? That was a case study in "if it ain't broke, don't fix it." Luckily, Coke had the wisdom to resurrect what had worked in the past and abandon the failed product. In contrast, as a society we can't seem to muster the courage to say "that didn't work" - we just keep trying to fix things.

As Christ-followers, we hold to time-honored biblical principles. Don't ever be ashamed or feel like you're not being progressive; sometimes progressive doesn't work. Romans 1:16 says, "For I am not ashamed of the gospel, because it is the power of God that brings salvation to everyone who believes: first to the Jew, then to the Gentile." Let's continue to be examples of Judeo-Christian values and maybe, just maybe, the world will take notice and say "You know, that works. We should give that a try again."

Father, many of us see the state of the world and sense that it is accelerating away from You. Help us to stand firm and not get caught up in the wake. Give us courage to stand for the Gospel and biblical principles in the face of "progressive thinking." Let us be lights that shine for You and bring You glory.

Monster Mash – Vampire Christianity

I grew up watching the old monster movies such as Bela Lugosi's *Dracula and* Lon Chaney's *The Wolf Man* and *Frankenstein*. I would sit up every Saturday night to watch Shock Theatre, hosted by Dr. Shock and his sidekick Dingbat. It was cheesy television at its best. I still remember the line as Dr. Shock signed off:

"And if you should awaken in the still of the night, the scream you hear may be your own."

Corny, I know, but it was effective on a 13-year-old who was up way past his bedtime. I still like an occasional scary movie, but Hollywood (as usual) has taken what used to be a somewhat harmless scare and turned it into some really hardcore depravity.

One of my favorites was the vampire genre. I remember the simple "vampire stare" by Bela Lugosi was enough to make me lie awake at night. In contrast, today's movies are infused with sex and more blood than the human body could even contain.

This may be a shaky analogy, but a recent article by Dallas Willard got me thinking about the concept of "Vampire Christianity." Vampires are called the "undead" and "creatures of the night." They need the blood of the living to survive, but they really have no desire to join the ranks of the living again.

I wonder how many of us fall into that category with our relationship with Christ. We recognize the power in His blood to save, but do we really want a complete transformation? Maybe we think that a little blood is enough for salvation, but we'd really like to hang onto our "creatures of the night" lifestyle.

The scriptures give us a different perspective. 2 Corinthians 5:17 says, "Therefore, if anyone is in Christ, he is a new creature; the old things passed away; behold, new things have come." There's no concept of hanging on to past lifestyle for the believer. If we continue to follow the vampire analogy, an encounter with Christ is like sunlight to the undead – there's nothing left but ashes of the old life. We're "born again" to a life free from the bondage of our previous sinful lifestyles.

There's a great old hymn that says "There is pow'r, pow'r, wondering working pow'r in the precious blood of the Lamb.[14]" It's hard to grasp the depths of the sacrifice that Christ endured to shed that precious blood on our behalf. There is salvation in the blood, but so much more.

It's a pathway to God the Father and eternal life. It's freedom from sin and despair. It's an opportunity to join in the great, timeless drama of creation. But it requires more than just a little blood. It requires obedience and dedication to an ongoing transformation into the likeness of Christ. And maybe a splash of garlic (wink)?

Father, help us to embrace the tremendous blessing of being a new creation. Help us to understand the scope and power in the shed blood of Christ. Transform us into men and women after Your own heart.

Monster Mash – The Walking Dead

The monster genre that I find particular disturbing is the zombie movie. Zombies are mindless former humans that exist only to eat…and I'll leave it at that. Zombies were always scary, but when I was growing up, at least you could outrun them. I see in modern zombie flicks, zombies can run! C'mon Hollywood, at least give us poor humans a chance.

One of the most popular TV shows airing now is *The Walking Dead*. It's a zombie apocalypse series focusing on a small band of survivors dodging zombies around every corner. I like a good "overcoming the odds" storyline, but the gore is over the top.

Think about the term "walking dead" for a moment. That is a perfect description of our lives prior to Christ. Ephesians 2:1 says, "As for you, you were dead in your transgressions and sins." So, we're spiritually dead, but we don't know it; we just keep walking around like everything is fine. Sounds like the definition of "walking dead" to me.

It's interesting how many monster genres portray the monster as "dead" but still interacting with the land of the living. Vampires are the "undead." Mummies are resurrected from the dead, but they're still cloth-wrapped, rotten bodies. Ghosts are dead, but still make their presence known to the living. It appears that, unbeknownst to them, Hollywood is showing us the truth of the human condition before Christ – we're dead in our sins.

That also leads to another perspective: there's nothing a dead person can do to come back to life. After all, he's dead. Similarly, we can't do anything to be "reborn" and experience life again. There's no amount of good deeds, giving to charity, or positive thinking that can remove the blanket of sin from our souls.

That's why Christ came. Ephesians 2:4 says, "But because of his great love for us, God, who is rich in mercy, made us alive with Christ even when we were dead in transgressions" and in verses 8-9, "For it is by grace you have been saved, through faith—and this is not from yourselves, it is the gift of God— not by works, so that no one can boast." God brings us back to life when we accept Christ as Savior. Undeserved forgiveness for the undead – only God can do that.

Father, thank You for the life that we have through Christ. Thank You for the opportunity to know You and follow You. You are the giver of life. Help us to cherish every day and use it for Your Kingdom.

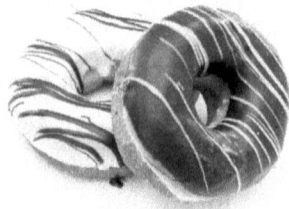

Monster Mash – I Need a Hero

Remember when the good guy always won? Our hero would fight against the creature with superior abilities, but find some way to overcome the odds and defeat evil. Dr. Van Helsing kept Dracula at bay with a cross until he could plant the stake, and the world was once again safe. We even felt bad for some monsters, such as Frankenstein's monster, but in the end, evil was still vanquished.

Well, in modern cinema, that concept has been defenestrated.[15] Remember the first movie you saw where the bad guy won?

"Wait… what!?!? That's it? (insert dumbfounded pause) Noooo way! It can't end like that!"

There are many variations of the villain's triumph in modern cinema. Probably the most devious are the ones that end with you thinking that the good guy won…and then the hand comes out of the water, or the monster's body is missing, or a light flickers to give you just enough doubt to wonder if the boogeyman is gone or not. Entire franchises have been formed around the monster that never dies – *Nightmare on Elm Street* and *Halloween* come to mind. I lost track of how many ridiculous *Friday the 13th* sequels there were.

And then there's the version where nobody wins. The hero is mistaken for the villain and both are killed, the whole city is nuked to stamp out the evil, or the entire planet is exterminated. Even when the hero wins, he's had to go to such extreme lengths, he can't live with himself when the deed is done.

Whenever I happen to see a movie where evil wins, I feel cheated…maybe even a bit violated.

61

Why the shift? I'm sure Hollywood would tell you that it's just trying to mimic real life. It's true that evil does win the occasional battle, but Hollywood has almost turned it into a coin flip. We could probably examine and argue the motivations all day, but what really matters is this…we know how the story ends. The history of man is a great drama played out on the stage of time. It has a beginning and a middle, and we're building toward the end. I have good news – the Good Guy wins!

Philippians 2:9-11 says, "Therefore God exalted him to the highest place and gave him the name that is above every name, that at the name of Jesus ever,y knee should bow, in heaven and on earth and under the earth, and every tongue acknowledge that Jesus Christ is Lord, to the glory of God the Father." Revelation 20:10 tells us that Satan, THE monster, will be cast into the lake of fire.

Take heart, child of God, even though the bad guy occasionally wins in today's world, there is a time coming when God will wipe away every tear and cast out all the monsters forever. And even though I know the ending, I can't wait to see the show.

Father, we live in a world that seems to embrace evil a little more each day. We see it in the news, movies, and in our neighborhoods. Lord, give us strength to stand for what's right, knowing that in the end the Lord will return victoriously to stamp out evil forever. Come, Lord Jesus!

Monster Mash – The Monster Club

Monster movies are famous for their endless sequels. I think the Friday the 13th series went ten rounds. Unlike those never-ending sequels, this will be the final monster-based devotion, I promise. The focus here is more about childhood memories, so hang with me.

When I was in the fourth grade, I started the Monster Club. Never heard of it? Well, we were big in Sylvania, Alabama. Ten of us collaborated to create what I consider to be my most cherished childhood artifact – the Monster Club notebook.

The Monster Club notebook is a simple three-ring binder, but it holds some priceless memories. Each of us would create a "monster." For each entry, the author would draw a picture of their most inventive creature. On the flipside of the paper, the monster's story would be told complete with his special power and the havoc he had wreaked on mankind. Some of the best entries are below reproduced exactly as they appear in the Monster Club notebook. Of course, it helps to have the pictures:

- The Ilkud – The Ilkud is the prehistoric Easter Bunny of long ago. He found some dinosaur eggs and dropped one in the lava which made it red which was the first colored egg. He would through(sic) them at enemies and if they missed he would go hunt them.

- Netrosaurusber – Netrosaurusber eats 12 people a day. He has no body only a head. It was cut off because he killed a girl. Now he is trying to find the girl that cut off his head.

- Clodanodsnot – The Clodanodsnot came from one of the Great Pyramids. He is just like a vampire. He sucks out the blood. One of the most famous kills was when he killed John Smith[16] and died 3 seconds after.

Ah, the raw creativity in the mind of the child. In the 4th grade we were at the top of our game. We had conquered the multiplication tables and the state capitols were about to go down. It was a pure accumulation of simple knowledge and it was fun.

As we left that innocent time, we began to be introduced to more complex topics, and by the time we reached college, knowledge accumulation was one thing, but determining what the knowledge meant was a whole different ball of wax. Simple acceptance had to be replaced with critical thinking skills. In 1st grade I learned that 2+2=4. In my higher math classes, I watched a professor attempt to disprove that. Can I go back to the 4th grade now?

But this is the way things work, even in our spiritual lives. 1 Corinthians 13:11 says "When I was a child, I talked like a child, I thought like a child, I reasoned like a child. When I became a man, I put the ways of childhood behind me." We are expected to grow up – physically, mentally and spiritually.

Unfortunately, some people just want to hang on to being a kid. The writer of Hebrews was exasperated when he wrote "In fact, though by this time you ought to be teachers, you need someone to teach you the elementary truths of God's word all over again. You need milk, not solid food!"[17]

Living in the world is hard, but we must take on the difficulties of life head-on like adults. It's great to reminisce about the Monster Club and those simpler times, but we can't live there.

The mission of the Kingdom requires us to be mature followers of Christ. We must engage the culture on the difficult topics and point them to Christ while raising up the next generation of believers. These are the cherished keepsakes that we will reminisce on for eternity.

Father, give us wisdom to apply the knowledge that we accumulate. Help us to put aside childish things and time-wasters and be ever-focused on building the Kingdom.

Doughnut Bites

At the 1934 World's Fair in Chicago, the doughnut was billed as "the food hit of the Century of Progress."

With Great Power Comes Great Responsibility

Romans 12:3-8 communicates the truth that each believer is given spiritual gifts according to the Lord's will. Such gifts as teaching, prophecy, and service are mentioned specifically, but I don't believe the gifts listed in scripture are exhaustive. God may bestow gifts of music, art, business acumen, etc. Regardless of the gift, the purpose is the same…to care for and serve one another to the glory of God.

I believe I have the spiritual gift of "one-liners." A one-liner is a joke that can be delivered in a single statement. It's different than telling a joke; I usually butcher those. However, my mind is constantly listening to conversations waiting for the opportunity to throw in a good zinger. To create laughter is a powerful thing that can brighten a mood and possibly shift a person's course for the rest of the day. An old Irish proverb says it all – A good laugh and a long sleep are the two best cures for anything.

Of course, as Spider Man would say, "with great power comes great responsibility." The gifts that God bestows on the believer can be misused. For example, I also have the gift of administration. I have used this gift for kingdom purposes by planning conferences and mission projects. It would be a misuse of this gift to put together an intricate plan to steal a shopping cart (hypothetically speaking).

For the gift of humor, I have to be particularly careful to avoid the "cutting" or "jabbing" type that garners a laugh at the expense of others. I must also carefully weigh the impact of the humor. I may have to pass up a perfect opportunity to make my Sunday school class erupt in laughter because I know it will totally derail the teacher from his lesson.

Timing is crucial to a successful one-liner. The window is there and if it closes, it's gone forever. That means I have to make lightning-fast decisions concerning the appropriateness of the humor. I have to confess; sometimes I don't always make the right decision in that millisecond of judgment.

As a case in point, we were on a trip with another couple and happened upon a Krispy Kreme doughnut shop. To really understand the situation, you have to know how much I love Krispy Kreme doughnuts. And to top it off – the hot light was on! We made our purchase and went back to the car to partake in sugary consumption. In the middle of doughnut bliss, I blurted out a made-up word to describe the joy I was experiencing. I assumed it would be funny, but the humor was amplified by the timing of my friend taking a sip of chocolate milk.

Have you ever seen chocolate milk come out someone's nose before? I think I had spleen cramp from laughing so hard. In hindsight, my made-up word was probably not appropriate. I'd ask you to judge for yourselves, but my wife has forbidden the word from appearing in this devotion. She's probably right, but for a couple of doughnuts, I might just be persuaded to tell you.

So, how are you using your spiritual gifts? Do you know what they are? There are several good spiritual gift surveys on the internet to guide you. Once you know them, are you going to use them for His glory or your own personal gain? Remember, "with great power comes great responsibility."

Father, thank You for bestowing gifts on Your children. Help us to cultivate those gifts by walking closely with You and guide us to use them to build up those around us. Convict us when we misuse these gifts for our own purposes. Give us daily opportunities to use our gifts to bring You glory.

Love Letters

I'm blessed to have married my high-school sweetheart. Sonya and I started dating when I was 17 and she was 15. We dated for 5 years before I decided I couldn't live without her, so I put a ring on her finger. During that 5-year period, we had a few ups and downs. We broke up twice, mainly because I thought there might be greener pastures, so to speak. There weren't. The second time we broke up and I tried to waltz back in, she wouldn't have me.

Oh man, did I do some silly things to try to win her back. The pièce de résistance was a 40-yard sign that I hung on the football field so she would see it during a band practice. Nope, that didn't work either. Finally, the stars aligned and we got back together, this time for good.

During all the teenage drama of courting, we wrote letters to each other. That's right, teenagers; we couldn't just text or post our random thoughts. We actually had to sit down and write out our feelings. Handwritten notes: what a concept!

Much to my wife's chagrin, I saved a few of those letters. What seemed like perfectly reasonable, heart-felt emotions now makes for pretty good comedy. Even though they seem kind of silly now, I wouldn't trade them for the world. They are documented proof of our feelings for each other. When our relationship gets a little strained, as all do at some point, it's nice to pull out the letters and remind ourselves of the early passion that grew into a 25+ year marriage.

The Bible contains a collection of love letters as well. John 3:16 talks about God's love and his desire to redeem man through Christ. Paul's letters to the first century church contain reminders of God's love for us and practical teaching on how to draw closer to Him in that love relationship.

True, it's not a romantic love typically associated with a "love letter," but it is a love between Father and child, Creator and creation, and love for one another as brothers and sisters.

Plus, God's love letters can have the same impact as my wife's. When my relationship with God gets a little strained, I can refer to the scriptures and remind myself of His love: a love so deep that blood was shed to win me back. I love my wife, but it pales in comparison to the love that God has for me, and His letters are a constant reminder.

1 John 4:9-11 (NLT) says, "God showed how much he loved us by sending his one and only Son into the world so that we might have eternal life through him. This is real love—not that we loved God, but that he loved us and sent his Son as a sacrifice to take away our sins. Dear friends, since God loved us that much, we surely ought to love each other." It's a little long, but I'll bet I could stretch that across a football field.

Father, You love us with a love that we can barely comprehend. Thank You for Your love and the love letters in the Bible to serve as a constant reminder. Give us a passion to dive into Your Word and cultivate our relationship with You.

Holy Mistaken Identity, Batman

Have you ever walked up to someone that seemed familiar, but upon closer examination, they weren't who you expected? This happened to my wife on one of our family vacations in a very memorable way.

We were on a road trip and made a pit stop at McDonald's. Being overly efficient, my son and I ran inside for a pit stop while my wife and daughters stayed in the drive-through line to grab some McSnacks. As Austin and I caught back up to them in the drive thru line, I happened to notice there was an identical van to ours in the line.

When I got back in the car, my wife was laughing hysterically. It seems we weren't the only overly-efficient, minivan-driving, fast-food-hungry family at the golden arches that day. The other dad obviously wasn't paying attention and got in my van by mistake…all the way in…to the point of putting the seat belt on.

"Excuse me," my wife calmly said, "but I think you're in the wrong van."

Panic, embarrassment, and several double-takes ensued as the misplaced father came to the realization that he'd jumped in the wrong vehicle. When he finally composed himself, I must admit, he had a great line.

"Are you sure you're not my family?"

I'm sure both families laughed all the way to their destinations that day. I know mine did.

Mistaken identities can be humorous, but they can also get you into trouble. For example, my wife and I were at a Sunday school get together once doing the mingling thing (mingling is my wife's spiritual gift). After a while I found my wife in the kitchen and came up behind her to give her a hug. I was inches away from slipping my arms around her waist when I froze…this wasn't my wife. One of the ladies in the class had identical hair to my wife's and I wasn't paying close enough attention. That's my story and I'm sticking to it!

Family members should be people that we recognize, even from a distance. Does this apply to the family of God? Sometimes. Have you ever met someone and within a few minutes you feel a kindred spirit? After more time has passed, you may learn that person is also a believer. That kindred spirit you felt was the Holy Spirit.

On the flip side, have you known people that claim to be Christ-followers, but nothing about their actions or personalities confirm their allegiance to Christ?[18] That's a tricky one, because they may be new in the faith, but they may be wolves in sheep's clothing. I like to call them CHRINOs – CHRistians In Name Only. Be careful, CHRINOs may say all the right words, but if you let them in the passenger seat of your life, they may take you where you don't want to go.

Father, You've given us relationships with family, friends, and fellow believers. Help us to discern when those relationships are causing a negative impact on our relationship with You. Give us courage to walk away from people in our lives who draw us away from godly living.

Spiritual Fertilizer

When I was growing up, my family did some gardening. When I got old enough, I was expected to participate. Of course, back then I only ate hamburgers and chicken fingers, so I wasn't all that thrilled about helping with vegetables.

The bane of my existence was the tiller. It took a long time to get the hang of it; it felt like trying to hold back a hoard of bargain hunters on Black Friday. As the crops matured I picked beans, shucked corn, and dug potatoes. The picking was followed closely by the canning process. Whew, you couldn't be within a hundred yards of the house on sauerkraut day.

Now that I'm older, I'm fascinated by the whole growing process. I just like to watch things grow – plants, flowers, even my grass. I've started doing a little gardening of my own. I've called my parents on several occasions to get some tips on gardening that I should have learned while I was in the middle of the process.

Unfortunately, I live in a subdivision on a lot that doesn't get a lot of direct sunlight. I've had to resort to some five-gallon buckets on my back deck. They've been fairly successful – at least I don't have to wrestle with the tiller.

One interesting thing I've learned in my limited gardening experience is it's not so much about the soil that produces great results - it's more important what you feed them. I watched several YouTube videos in preparation for my foray into gardening. One gardener planted all his beds with a mixture of sand and sawdust. Now, I'm obviously no expert, but there are absolutely zero nutrients in that concoction. Instead of pulling nutrients from the soil, he had a special fertilizer that he used weekly to feed his plants.

Judging from his success, I decided to give his miracle fertilizer a try. I gathered the ingredients and mixed up the witch's brew – perlite, 10-10-10 fertilizer, eye of newt, and other miscellaneous minerals. I guess it's working – my corn and tomato plants are seven feet tall and I have more cucumbers than I know what to do with. Pretty good for a rookie with five-gallon buckets and limited sunlight, huh?

Think about your spiritual growth for a moment. You may face similar challenges – it's all new to you, you don't have a family that's supportive, or you don't have an opportunity to interface with other believers on a regular basis. You're planted in some less-than-desirable soil. But that shouldn't hinder your growth, because it's more about what you're being fed.

A steady dose of the scriptures and prayer and you have all you need to overcome a harsh growing environment. There's an old adage - "Bloom where you're planted." Regardless of the circumstances, you can produce fruit for the Kingdom. You just need a regular dose of spiritual fertilizer, and you'll be blooming in no time.

Father, help us to look past the difficulties of life and dedicate ourselves to growing closer to You. If there are weeds in our lives that choke out our growth, You have our permission to get the tiller out and take care of those distractions. It's all about You and producing fruit that the Master Gardener will be pleased with.

Doing Battle from the Man Bench

Never are the differences between the sexes on greater display than when the two go shopping.

Let me explain it from the male perspective. In general, men don't like to shop. When we do shop, we approach it as a hunting expedition. If I need a pair of brown shoes, I go to the first store I see, stalk the brown shoe aisle until I see a potential prey. I pounce on the shoe and try it on. If it fits, I'm done and I drag my kill to the cash register so it can be bagged and tagged.

Ladies, on the other hand, can turn shopping into a social event. They'll invite their friends, go browse random items whether they actually need anything or not. My wife will walk around and fill up a shopping cart with various items and when she's got it out of her system, just leave the cart and go home.

Visualize the typical shopping scenario with me. The husband will usually let the wife take the lead since this is her natural habitat. Men will pray for extra doses of patience while the wives proceed to pick up and examine every article of clothing in the store. Praise the Lord that He has shown mercy to men everywhere by leading store owners to create the greatest invention of all time – the man bench.

Yes, the man bench. A refuge for manhood found in malls all across America. Walk up to any man bench area and you'll hear a similar conversation:

"Hey."

"Hey."

"What're you in for?"

"The Gap. You?"

"Old Navy." With pleasantries out of the way, we both start reading our email on our smart phones. The silence will continue unless there's a disturbance in the Force.

"Look at that guy. He just went into Bed, Bath and Beyond with his wife."

"Poor guy must be a newlywed. He'll be out here with us soon enough. Well, good luck. My wife's waving at me. She needs the credit card."

Kidding aside, I'm grateful for the differences between my wife and me. She sees things in situations that I don't and vice versa.

God gave us instructions in Ephesians 5 for negotiating those differences in the Christian household. If I had to boil it down, a successful marriage is all about submitting to each other in love and putting each other first. Every day should be a fresh challenge for meeting each other's needs. Sounds simple, but judging from the out of control divorce rate, it's certainly not. Selfishness is in our nature and has to be battled every day.

Going shopping with our wives is a simple example, but in reality, we are placing our wives' desires and needs over our own. So, the next time you see guys on the man bench, just remember, they are doing battle for their relationships…and they are winning.

Father, thank You for our spouses. Let us take the words of Ephesians 5 to heart and place our spouses' needs before our own. Please bless and grow our relationships.

The End of the Internet

There are a few people in the world that I consider comedic geniuses – Robin Williams, Bill Cosby, the federal government, etc. In particular, Steve Martin was a big influence on my comedic development. I must have listened to his album *Wild and Crazy Guy* a million times. I can still quote the dialogue word for word.

I found Steve Martin on twitter the other day and his tweets are exactly the kind of dry wit that I would expect from him. A couple of examples:

"I have yet to meet a kind, witty, interesting, attractive, rich person I didn't like."

"Please don't make the mistake I did: Power BARS are what you eat; power STRIPS are what you plug into."

"There. I finally read the internet."

That last one reminded me of a contracting job I held a few years ago. I left my job of 11 years to chase a lucrative contract that was being dangled in front of my resume'. It was an okay job, but after about three months they ran out of things for me to do. I asked what I should be working on and the response was, "Just do some research and learn a little more about the industry." Translation – we don't know; just go surf the internet.

Sounds like a dream job, right? It was kinda nice…for the first few days. I don't know if you've ever gone for a long stretch with not much to at work, but after a month it was beginning to get old. I remember the day I got home and announced to my family:

"I didn't think it could be done, but I have reached the end of the internet."

I literally could not think of anything else to look up online. I was bored out of my mind. It was bad enough that I was being paid to goof off, but my company continued to bill the client at my ridiculous rate. I soon parted ways with my "dream job."

God created us to work. It wasn't a consequence of the fall of man that we had to work; that was always the plan.[19] As a Christ-follower, we're not only supposed to work, but to bring God glory while we do it. 1 Corinthians 10:31 says, "So whether you eat or drink or whatever you do, do it all for the glory of God."

Everything we undertake, including our jobs, should be done for His glory. Also, in Colossians 3:23 it says, "Whatever you do, work at it with all your heart, as working for the Lord, not for human masters." That tells me that my job is not about "working for the man" - it's about working for the "Son of Man." I should be working as if Jesus himself were my boss.

Knowing that I wasn't earning my wage and that there was some shady client billing going on, I just couldn't stay in that job anymore. Luckily I landed on my feet fairly quickly. In Steve Martin's case, that would be "happy feet!"

Father, give us a fresh perspective of our jobs. Even if our bosses are pains in the neck, let us look pass them and see You as our ultimate boss. Lord, give us the opportunity each day to shine for You at work in a way that will make others ask questions. And help us to be ready with the right answers.

The Proof is in the Fruit

One of the most famous trials in recent American history was the O.J. Simpson murder trial. It was the first trial that I can remember that became a true media circus. The prosecutor got a makeover. The detective, Mark Furman, has made a career out of his involvement with the case. Unfortunately, the only thing missing from the proceedings was the anticipated guilty verdict and O.J. was declared not guilty.

The most dramatic scene of the trial involved a pair of bloody gloves that were worn by the murderer. In a stroke of legal genius, the lead defense attorney, Johnny Cochran, requested that O.J. try on the gloves. In a dramatic struggle with the glove, O.J. declared that the glove would not go on his hand. This led to the famous line by Johnny Cochran to the jury:

"If the glove doesn't fit, you must acquit!"

Evidence is critical in any criminal trial. Did you know that God considers evidence important as well? James 2:14-25 is a passage that talks about faith and works. James' point in this passage is this – vindicate your faith by your works. It's not enough to just claim that you are a Christ-follower, it's important to show it through your deeds.

The Bible also refers to these works as fruit. Consider this passage in Matthew 7:16-20 where Jesus warns about false teachers – "By their fruit you will recognize them. Do people pick grapes from thornbushes, or figs from thistles? Likewise, every good tree bears good fruit, but a bad tree bears bad fruit. A good tree cannot bear bad fruit, and a bad tree cannot bear good fruit. Every tree that does not bear good fruit is cut down and thrown into the fire. Thus, by their fruit you will recognize them."

That sounds like examining evidence to me. If we tried to defend our faith in a court of law, would there be enough evidence to prove our case? Are there instances of sacrificial giving, pure living and service to our brothers and sisters to make our case? Are there times of Bible study and prayer that we can point to as evidence of our devotion? Is there fruit or would the prosecution have cause to say:

"If the fruit is not there, then CHRINO beware!"[20]

Our salvation is by God's grace alone; there's nothing we can do to earn it.[21] But He does expect us to bear fruit as evidence of that salvation. It's always a good idea to do some personal fruit inspection to determine if we are producing the fruit that God has already prepared for us.[22] Be assured, we will face the Judge one day. We better have our evidence ready to present.

Father, thank You for the opportunities You provide for us to bear fruit. Make us focused and diligent to look for those opportunities when they present themselves. Forgive us when we get so wrapped up in the temporal things of life that we miss the simple things that last for eternity.

Much Harm, No Foul?

In high school I was a member of the basketball team. It was great opportunity to be a part of a team and feel the sense of accomplishment as we strove together to reach for victory (insert triumphant fanfare).

Yeah, I'm sure it was about that, but it was mainly to get the girls' attention. And how could we not garner the attention of the ladies with our sexy knee-high tube socks and shorts that barely covered our underwear? Please, please tell me no one has any pictures of those uniforms (shudder).

Every year our team would travel to a local college for basketball camp. This was a week dedicated to honing our skills, learning to work as a team, and testing our mettle against other teams at the camp (obviously, no girls at camp).

Side note – the college didn't bother to turn on the boilers during the summer; there was zero hot water…nada. As you can imagine, taking a shower was mandatory after sweating all day. It was easy to tell when your neighbor got in the shower because you could hear him shout "Woo hooo hooooo!" It was an uncontrollable reaction to being pelted with 33 degree water.

During one of the scrimmages, we played against a team with one player who was an imposing presence. I don't remember the team name, I don't remember if we won or lost, but I will never forget…Cirillo.

Cirillo, who may or may not have a first name, was a beast on the court. A giant of a man, he played at another level than the rest of us mere mortals. During one particular trip down the court I pulled up for a long jump shot. Out of nowhere, Cirillo leaped to block my shot. He successfully blocked the shot, I'm pretty sure with his knees, and proceeded to flatten me into a greasy spot on the court.

All I remember after that is half my team yelling at the ref for not calling a foul and the other half making sure all my limbs were still attached. To this day, my former teammates can simply walk up behind me and say "Cirillo" and in true Pavlovian fashion, I flinch.

Do you have a "Cirillo" event in your past - something that really knocked you for a loop and still causes you to cringe when it comes to mind? Can I offer you a verse of comfort when those past anxieties come flooding back? Philippians 4:6-8 (NASB) says, "Be anxious for nothing, but in everything by prayer and supplication with thanksgiving let your requests be made known to God. And the peace of God, which surpasses all comprehension, shall guard your hearts and your minds in Christ Jesus. Finally, brethren, whatever is true, whatever is honorable, whatever is right, whatever is pure, whatever is lovely, whatever is of good repute, if there is any excellence and if anything worthy of praise, let your mind dwell on these things."

It takes discipline, but if you can train your mind to think on the things of God, instead of the things of the past, the scriptures promise peace that we can't even comprehend.

One method to refocus your mind on God is to "count your blessings." Mentally or physically list the myriad of ways God has blessed you. After a while, you'll experience the peace of God and your "Cirillo" will be back in the past where he belongs.

Father, thank You for Your peace. Teach us to turn our minds and our hearts to You and remind us how much You love us. Give us relief from old memories that plague us and replace them with Your mercies that are new every morning.

Lessons from the Trading Floor – Take Time to Disconnect

I used to work for an energy company that engaged in real-time trading of energy – like Enron, but without all the criminal activity. A company that participates in real-time trading must always be connected so that communication is near-instantaneous. That's why we all worked on a trading floor about the size of an arena football field, just me and 400 of my closest "friends." There were real-time prices posted on big ticker boards and four jumbotrons on each end of the floor to pipe in the Weather Channel, CNN, or any other news source that might impact trading.

Some of my coworkers thrived in this environment, but I didn't particularly care for it. There was absolutely no downtime. You were always connected to your surroundings. Sometimes it was the Wild West. For example:

"LANE, WHY IS THE TRADING SYSTEM DOWN?" shouts my primary user from the other end of the floor.

Eight hundred curious eyes look up and wait for my response. Of course, I don't yell back. I calmly walk over and figure out what the problem is – usually, it was a user error. On the way back I want to say "Crisis averted, citizens. Return to your computer monitors, nothing to see here."

One of the perks to being on the floor was around the time of the NCAA Basketball tournament. The games are televised during the afternoon on Thursday and Friday, so the traders merged the jumbotron into one giant screen to get their March Madness on. We'd be working away and then someone would make a game-winning shot. You'd hear half the floor in unison say, "Ohh!" The other half of the floor, startled, would look up to see what happened. Fun stuff.

However, I found that being "always connected" could be exhausting. Sometimes I would steal away to a conference room just to get away from the floor roar. As a software developer, it was necessary to get in the zone and do some heavy thinking.

Sometimes I would catch myself staring into space trying to solve a coding dilemma when I realize I've been looking directly at a coworker across the floor who wondered why I was staring at him. Queue the quick head turn.

Jesus also knew what it was like to be "always connected." By the time His ministry was in full swing, He couldn't go anywhere without attracting a crowd. However, Jesus knew the importance of disconnecting for a season.[23] Mark 6:31 says "Then, because so many people were coming and going that they did not even have a chance to eat, he said to them, 'Come with me by yourselves to a quiet place and get some rest.'"

In today's society, social media has taken being "connected" to a whole new level. We can know everything that is going on across the planet, plus what everyone on the planet thinks about it. It's both exhilarating and exhausting. We have to be able to give ourselves permission to disconnect. Let's put down the smart phones and be smart about our spiritual lives. Spend time in the Word meditating on His majesty. You might look up to find that your spirit is staring directly into the eyes of His Spirit. Hold that gaze for a while.

Father, we live in a world of non-stop information. Help us to remember that the timeless information found in Your Word is far more worthy of our attention. Lord, give us a fresh desire to know You and find a quiet place to meditate on You.

Lessons from the Trading Floor – Making a Good Bet

Working for a real-time energy trading company, traders were called on to make educated guesses about how to price energy so it would be purchased. There were lots of variables – weather, cost of fuel, historical prices, etc. But after all that is taken into consideration, there was still an element of chance involved.

So, as you can imagine, the traders had a natural bent toward games of chance. I witnessed several instances of gambling. In fact, those guys would wager on just about anything – basketball brackets, pools to predict the date of a child's birth, etc.

If there wasn't a sporting event or something normal to bet on, they'd just make stuff up. My favorites involved the consumption of a food in a predetermined time period. This was not Fear Factor level of grossness, but it wasn't far behind.

One bet involved consuming an entire stick of butter in 60 seconds. Everyone kicked in $10 until the pot was big enough to lure the prey to attempt the task. The clock started and he began to methodically slice the stick into bite-sized patties. He did it…and the floor erupted in applause. On another occasion, the bet was to drink an entire bottle of olive oil in 60 seconds. I can't imagine how that impacted his digestive system.

The most interesting by far involved a guy on the floor who was a multiple sneezer. When he started sneezing, everyone looked up. At the fourth sneeze, everyone started counting…out loud. If he made it past seven, the floored cheered. If not, the floor booed. In either case, money changed hands. I never understood the details of that bet, but it was obvious when a trader made a bad bet.

Gambling is all about choosing a bet that gives you the best odds of winning. Sounds like a job for a mathematician. Seventeenth century mathematician Blaise Pascal quantified the odds for and against betting on Christianity. His argument is known as Pascal's Wager.[24] Let me give you my version of Pascal's Wager in the following decision matrix:

	God is real / Christianity is true	God is not real / Christianity is false
I follow Christ	WIN – eternal life and heaven (jackpot)	DRAW – Life is all there is. I've lived a moral life and been associated with likeminded people
I do not follow Christ	LOSE – eternal separation from God in Hell	DRAW – Life is all there is. I've lived my life based on my own moral code and associated with likeminded people

As you can see, according to the decision matrix, following Christ is the logical course of action. The worst possible outcome is that I've lived a good life for no reason. But I would want my life to be lived this way regardless. Not following Christ is a wager where the stakes could not be higher. For someone to hear the gospel and turn away, they are going "all in" with their souls. That's not a bet I'm willing to make.

Father, we take calculated risks every day, from buying life insurance to deciding if the milk is ruined. Thank You for a mind that is able to reason and make these decisions. Lord, help us explain to our neighbors the risks and rewards of following You. Open their eyes of faith and help them see that following You is the best bet.

Gravesite Evasion

"Ooh, I just got a chill up my spine."

"That means someone just walked over your grave."

The first time someone told me that old wive's tale, I was pretty young and it spooked me a little bit. The phrase comes from medieval times when walking on a gravesite was thought to be disrespectful, and if you deliberately did so, it meant you wished something bad to happen to them.

Respecting and visiting the graves of departed family members was a part of the rural southern culture in which I was raised. Every Sunday in the month of May was set aside for "Decoration." Decoration was an event where people would congregate at cemeteries to visit the graves of departed family members and place flower arrangements out of respect. It was a social event as well, giving people a chance to visit with friends they may not have seen for a long time. As morbid as it sounds, it's a nice tradition.

This is where I was trained in the guerrilla warfare technique of gravesite evasion. As a young lad, I was taught to respect a gravesite and not walk across it. That's a little trickier than it sounds in some cemeteries. Sometimes the headstones and footstones are hard to find. Sometimes the graves are not lined up neatly beside each other, requiring some wild zigzagging to get from place to place. It felt like negotiating a mine field; one misstep and "BAM" - you just sent a chill up some unsuspecting guy's spine. This was serious stuff, folks!

Here's another good reason to not walk across a gravesite. 1 Thessalonians 4:16 says, "For the Lord Himself will descend from heaven with a shout, with the voice of an archangel, and with the trumpet of God. And <u>the dead in Christ will rise first</u>." I don't know about you, but when Christ returns and the dead start coming out of the graves, I don't want to be standing on some long-departed saint's head who's trying to get to the Savior. Awkward!

Luckily, I won't be far behind him because verse 17 continues, "Then we who are alive and remain shall be caught up together with them in the clouds to meet the Lord in the air. And thus we shall always be with the Lord." No more death, no more pain, no more graves to dodge…that's going to be a great day! I get a chill up my spine just thinking about it.

Father, we look forward with great hope to Your return. We long for the days when all our cares will be left behind as we streak through the air to meet You. Maranatha![25]

Spiritual Kudzu

If you've ever spent any time in the South, you've probably seen kudzu. Kudzu is a Japanese vine that was introduced to the United States in 1876. Now, it's everywhere. It is appropriately nicknamed "the vine that ate the south." It moves from tree to tree, choking out entire forests.

But did you know that kudzu was once considered a beneficial plant that the government promoted planting? In the 30's and 40's the plant was actively used to prevent soil erosion. Farmers planted over a million acres before the light bulb came on: there's no stopping this stuff. It was recognized as a pest weed in the 1950s and removed from the list of acceptable species in the Agricultural Conservation Program. In 1998, it was listed as a federal noxious weed by the U.S. Congress.[26]

In many ways, kudzu is an excellent metaphor for sin in the life of the believer. It seems harmless and looks pretty, but once it takes hold, it chokes out any further growth. Consider the progression of kudzu – it was perceived to have benefits such as erosion control and ornamental beauty, and some alternative medicine sources tout its medicinal value.[27] However, the danger came from not keeping it in check and soon the destructive power of kudzu far outweighed its benefits.

Sin can take the same path in the life of the believer. Consider alcohol or marijuana – there are some medicinal values in the antioxidants of wine and marijuana has been proven to be an effective drug to treat glaucoma. However, both of these substances can move from beneficial to destructive in a short amount of time.

So my question is – why play with fire? I don't play video games anymore because I can become completely consumed by them and spend countless hours trying to free a princess from some digital boogeyman. In the same vein, I wouldn't plant kudzu in my backyard for erosion control. That stuff can grow up to a foot a day. Before I realize it, it's taken over. It's just not worth the risk.

Be honest with yourself; you know what your spiritual kudzu is. You know where your weak area is and what has the potential of taking over your life. The only way to kill kudzu is to destroy the root system. It's not enough to trim it or even cut it off at the ground; it will come back.

In the same way, there are some areas of our lives that cutting back is not enough; it takes a complete eradication. The only way to do that is by a complete transformation of the mind through the Holy Spirit.[28] Regular Bible study and prayer are the only surefire pesticides for spiritual kudzu.

Father, show us the areas of our lives that are being choked out by sin. Give us the courage to remove those sins completely from our lives. Strengthen us daily to walk in a manner worthy of You.

What's in a Name?

"Lane, could you read Genesis chapter 10 for us?"

When I reach the passage I make a quick survey. Uh oh. My brow furrows. A bead of sweat starts to form on my temple. I'm about to tackle a genealogy list...out loud. I remember some words of advice from a former pastor – "Just take your best shot and keeping moving." I put on my trusty hooked-on-phonics helmet and I'm off.

I get past Gomer, Magog and Javan; it looks like I'm going to make it. Then the train jumps the tracks when I attempt Ashkenaz, Riphath and Togarmah. I'm not Pentecostal, but I'm pretty sure I'm speaking in tongues. By the time I reach the last begat I'm drenched in sweat. I need to lie down.

Why are biblical names so difficult to pronounce? I remember when I was a kid my pastor preached a sermon on Mephibosheth. He knew he was going to struggle with the pronunciation so he prepared a sign with the name printed on it. When his tongue failed him, he just held up the sign like a white flag.

It's a good thing we don't live in biblical times, because they apparently took pronunciation very seriously. For example, forty-two thousand Ephraimites were killed because they couldn't pronounce "Shibboleth."[29] I'm glad we don't observe that today; I'd have to pop a cap in about 90% of the people I meet because they can't pronounce my last name.

So, why all the names in the Bible? Be honest, we don't spend a lot of time on those passages, right? We just kind of skim them. I think the Lord will forgive us for not meditating on those verses too long. But they were important enough to include for a couple of reasons.

One obvious reason is to prove the divine and royal lineage of Christ. But think about the second reason for a moment – simply the fact that God knew their name. The living God, the creator of the universe, chooses to have personal relationships with His creation. He knew their name...and He knows your name. That's pretty astounding when you think about it.

Names carried more significance in biblical times than they do today. Names actually meant something. For example Isaac means "laughter" because Sarah laughed at the thought of having a child at her age. Abraham means "father of a great multitude."

The Jewish people hold the name of God in such high esteem, they will not even speak it aloud. In Hebrew the name consists of four letters and is written יהוה. Theologians call it the Tetragrammaton, a fancy word which simply means "word of four letters" (go impress your friends at the next party). We would pronounce יהוה as Yahweh or Jehovah.

What's in a name? How about this - Jesus means "savior, deliverer." Philippians 2:8-11 says, "And being found in appearance as a man, he humbled himself by becoming obedient to death - even death on a cross! Therefore God exalted him to the highest place and gave him the name that is above every name, that at the name of Jesus every knee should bow, in heaven and on earth and under the earth, and every tongue acknowledge that Jesus Christ is Lord, to the glory of God the Father." That's a name I want to be associated with.

Father, give us a renewed reverence for the majesty of Your name. As we bear the name of Christ, allow us to feel the weight of that responsibility. Help us to make your name known throughout the earth.

"Always end the name of your child with a vowel, so that when you yell the name will carry." - Bill Cosby

Trivia question: What is the longest name in the Bible? The answer is located in this endnote.[30]

Doughnuts with Dad

It's a typical Monday. The alarm goes off at 5:30AM. After a few moments of denial, I have to crank up the Jaws of Life to free me from the self-indulgent bonds of sleep. Soon I'm in my car quickly making my way to the interstate so I can secure my place in line with the 15 quadrillion cars commuting to work in Atlanta traffic.

My mind is swarming with things I need to accomplish at work today. I get to my desk, acquire the first cup of coffee, and prepare to dive into a cornucopia of issues that needs to be resolved.

"Ring." It's my wife calling. When she calls this early in the morning it usually means I forgot something. Today would be no different.

"Did you forget that today is Doughnuts with Dad at Cassidy's preschool?"

My heart stops. Cassidy has been looking forward to this for days. This is bad, really bad. All the plans for the day are violently pushed aside and replaced with a single purpose – I have to get to my daughter! I find my boss and tell him I'll be back later and soon I am speeding back home.

I'm pretty sure I broke every traffic law and some new ones that will probably be named after me. I thought I was going to make it on time, but due to an obvious red-light conspiracy, I was a few minutes late. The program had begun. When I burst into the room every child was standing in a large circle around the room with their dad standing beside them. In the center of the room was my daughter sitting by herself.

In that moment, when our eyes met, we shared two diametrically opposed views. In her eyes I could see that I was her hero; a knight in shining armor charging in to scoop her up and join her friends in the circle. If she were mature enough, she might have been able to read my eyes as well. She would have seen tears forming in the eyes of the worst father on the planet – at least that's how I felt.

On this fateful day, as I drowned my sorrows in more than my share of doughnuts, I made the decision to re-double my efforts to be there for my kids. Unfortunately, this would not be the last time I would disappoint my daughter, or my other two children. There have been missed ballgames and concerts that I'll never get back. Oh, I made it to almost every event, but the time we have as parents is so short, it seems a shame to miss any of them.

Aren't you glad that we have a Savior that never misses an event and never disappoints? Jesus said in Matthew 28:20, "Surely I am with you always, to the very end of the age."

Have you ever felt like you're that person in the middle of the circle? Everyone seems to be participating, but you're just sitting by yourself? Can I offer some encouragement? Jesus is there. He cares for you and He's ready to burst through the door and scoop you up into His arms.

Father, thank You for being a continuous presence in our lives. You don't turn away when we screw up, but instead wait patiently for us to return to Your sheltering wing. Draw us close, Father, and give us the peace of knowing You.

Muscle Quest – The Physical

There's something you need to know about me to get the correct visual for this story (although I'm not sure I want you to visualize this). I was kinda slim growing up. OK, let's be honest, I was "somebody-get-that-kid-a-sandwich" skinny when I was young. When I graduated high school I was 5'10" and weighed 120 pounds, soaking wet. Charles Atlas approached me to be the poster child for the "98 pound weakling." OK, I might be exaggerating a little, but suffice it to say, I was not known for my physique.

As a result, I endured the traditional bullying and taunting from those blessed with more muscle mass. This drove me to try and "bulk up" on several occasions. I've learned several lessons from weightlifting:

Always make sure the last guy wipes the equipment off before you lie down (gross).

Always use a spotter. I learned this after failing to complete a bench press...at home...by myself. You don't have a lot of time to consider escape scenarios when you're pinned to the bench by more weight than you can lift.

Luckily, I didn't put the clasps on the end of the bars, so I could slowly lower one end until the weights fell off. Of course, that caused the weights on the other end to whip over and violently crash to the ground on the other side.

Always use a spotter (did I mention that?). Same lesson, but not me this time. I was in the gym with one other guy who was doing squats. He had six, 45-pound plates on each side of the bar (you do the math).

This guy was a beast, or at least he thought he was. He placed a bench behind him, the idea being he would squat down to the bench and then stand up to complete the rep. Well, he squatted…and just sat down. He couldn't get off the bench. He started yelling for help.

Did I mention I was the only other person working out? The guy who worked at the gym came running out when he heard the commotion. He quickly sized up the situation, took one look at me, and ran out of the room looking for someone else to help him free the pinned squatter. Upon return with help, they took off enough plates to release Conan from his iron prison. I think the only injury that day was his pride.

Don't take pills without asking lots of questions. As part of my quest to become Mr. Olympia, I visited a "weight doctor" that specialized in strength and fitness. He gave me some meds that were supposed to help with weight gain, but warned that I should work out vigorously while taking them.

I took his advice and worked out like never before, and it worked. Within two weeks the muscles in my chest had grown significantly. All my friends were noticing. It was awesome!

Then my Mom got suspicious. On the follow-up visit, she asked exactly what these meds were. "Oh, they're anabolic steroids," he answered coolly. Of course, that was my last visit to the "weight doctor." The pills stopped and within a week my newfound man-chest was replaced with the normal 16-year-old-boy chest. Thanks a lot, Mom!

As I've gotten older, the self-consciousness about my physique is all but gone. I'm more concerned with just having a healthy lifestyle, not packing on the muscle. I now know that my value as a man is not in my appearance or my physical strength, it's actually more dependent on my weakness.

Paul said in 2 Corinthians 12:10, "That is why, for Christ's sake, I delight in weaknesses, in insults, in hardships, in persecutions, in difficulties. For when I am weak, then I am strong." That's a complete one eighty to the world's perspective.

I'm thankful that my entrance into Heaven is not dependent on my own strength. Instead, it is dependent on the strength of a Savior that carried a heavy cross up a path to Golgotha and bore the weight of not only my sin, but the sin of the entire world. Now, that's what I called serious weightlifting!

Father, You've given us wonderful bodies made in Your image. Help us to have a healthy self-image and realize that we are designed by Your hand for your purpose. Keep our primary focus on spiritual health as we maintain a healthy body.

Muscle Quest – The Spiritual

I learned a valuable lesson recently – never trust a pastor that says "Hey, can you help me with an illustration?" At least, be sure to ask questions before blindly agreeing. The venue for this life lesson was a father/son camping trip. Our Minister to Adults was slated to give the devotion that night. He asked me that fateful question and I said, "Sure, whatever you need." Oh boy, was that a mistake.

We all gathered around the campfire that night with our sons, who were much more interested in finding anything remotely flammable to throw in the fire. After coaxing the budding arsonists away from the flames, the devotion began. The topic was about building "spiritual muscles." That's when I started to regret not asking more questions.

Our Minister to Adults asked his five volunteers to join him near the campfire and form a line. At the count of three, we were instructed to get shirtless and give the group our best Mr. Universe "pose down." Before anyone had time to object, the countdown began. Shirts started flying, so, of course, I had to play along.

As I alluded to in a previous devotion, I've never been mistaken for Arnold Schwarzenegger, so this kind of activity was sure to open me up to some light-hearted ribbing. Well, let me tell you, Arnold would have been proud of our effort. You'd have thought we were all seasoned bodybuilders. Muscles clenched, faces grimaced, and the crowd went wild.

Fortunately for me, our speaker had also chosen an older gentleman to participate and he stole the show. He was wearing a wooly sweater before the posing began. When he took it off, well, he was as wooly as the sweater. I don't know if bodybuilding has a senior wolfman division, but this guy would be a shoo-in.

The idea behind the illustration was that guys spend a lot more time focused on physical strength than building spiritual muscle. Paul puts the two in perspective - 1 Timothy 4:8 says, "For physical training is of some value, but godliness has value for all things, holding promise for both the present life and the life to come."

According to Paul, we shouldn't neglect the physical; it's perfectly fine to hit the gym and get in shape. However, the time we spend building our physical bodies should pale in comparison to the commitment to building our spiritual strength.

Hmm, I wonder what a spiritual pose down would look like. I'm going to think on that for a while so I can get the mental image of the geriatric Sasquatch out of my mind.

Father, help us to spend as much time concerned about our inner selves as the outer. Allow us to see our bodies as the temporary shells that they are. Give us a passion for building the spiritual strength required to serve You and bring You glory.

Muscle Quest – No Pain, No Gain

You've heard the expression "no pain, no gain." When I think of that phrase I picture a guy struggling to complete that last repetition of a bench press with his spotter barking commands to "Push!" There really is pain involved because resistance training causes small tears in the muscle fibers.

Most people think they are building muscles in the gym, but, in reality, they're breaking down the muscles during a workout. The muscles grow during the resting time as the body knits those tears back together.[31]

There are many parallels when it comes to building spiritual muscle. First, we need resistance to work the muscles. In the gym, that comes in the form of dumbbells, pushups or squats. In the spiritual realm, our faith is strengthened by the three T's - trials, tests and temptations. And just like a strenuous workout, the three Ts can cause some real pain. Let's drill down a little farther on each:

Trials

Life is hard. Trials are those things that happen in all our lives just because we're still breathing. My child has the flu. I lost my job. My hybrid car batteries died and will cost me $3,000 to replace (purely hypothetical, of course). 1 Peter 4:12-13 says, "Dear friends, do not be surprised at the fiery ordeal that has come on you to test you, as though something strange were happening to you. But rejoice inasmuch as you participate in the sufferings of Christ, so that you may be overjoyed when his glory is revealed." If I tie this back to the physical analogy – sometimes you just have to climb a set of stairs, or cut the grass, or clean the house. These things are just going to happen and they build muscle along the way.

Tests

Sometimes the source of difficulty comes directly from God. In Genesis, we read accounts where God tested Abraham.[32] If we don't look at this with the right perspective, this can make God look like the bad guy.

In these situations, I think of God as our personal trainer. He's the spotter urging us to "Push!," knowing that we are growing stronger as a result. He's right there, giving us just enough help to complete the repetition. If we fail, He's there to remove the weight. He won't give us more than we can bear, but He expects us to give it all we have.

Temptations

We have an enemy in the world and he looks for opportunities to trip us up. If Satan can cause us to sin, it damages our relationship with the Father. It separates us from our Trainer and takes us out of the gym, much like a physical injury would.

Or maybe it's as simple as "I'm just too tired to go to the gym today." One day turns into two and soon you've gone from fit to fat. It's the same kind of temptation in the spiritual realm – "I just don't feel like reading my Bible today." Before long it's been days since you've been in the Word.

The good news is that God gives us strength to resist the temptation. 1 Corinthians 10:13 says, "No temptation has overtaken you except what is common to mankind. And God is faithful; he will not let you be tempted beyond what you can bear. But when you are tempted, he will also provide a way out so that you can endure it."

When I think of this, I see God as our trainer in a boxing match. As we're doing battle with the enemy, he's giving us encouragement, patching us up, and telling us how to deflect the enemy's blows. If God be for us, who can be against us?[33]

Woe is us, the three Ts are out to get us, right? The Bible has a different take. James 1:2-3 says, "Consider it pure joy, my brothers and sisters, whenever you face <u>trials</u> of many kinds, because you know that the <u>testing</u> of your faith produces perseverance. Let perseverance finish its work so that you may be mature and complete, not lacking anything." Pure joy. That's what is says, pure joy.

Athletes will tell you something similar. When they really push themselves, there's a "high" that they get from the exertion and the satisfaction of knowing that they've pushed beyond their boundaries. That's the same joy we should feel from trials, tests and overcoming temptations. The Spirit will fill us completely as we draw our strength from Him and we will become more like Christ. I think that's the kind of gain that's worth the pain.

Father, thank You for the trials of life. They aren't fun, but they're necessary for our growth. Give us strength to overcome and forgive us when we fail. Build our spiritual muscles, Lord. Make us more like Christ each day.

Lazy Tales – Get Your Head Out of Bed

If I had to list my vices I'm afraid laziness would be near the top. There's an endless list of productive things I could be doing, but all too often I choose the appropriately named La-Z-Boy.

One area of laziness that I struggle with is sleeping late. I've always been a night owl, so dragging myself out of bed in the morning has always been a particular challenge for me. Unfortunately, the Atlanta commute is not kind to the person who gets a late start. In Atlanta, the early bird doesn't get the worm; he gets to work in less than 2 hours. As a result, my alarm is set for the unthinkable time of 5:30AM.

Assuming I successfully navigate the interstate craziness, I arrive at my office with a single thought on my mind – "Must have coffee." Don't even try to carry on a conversation with me until the java is coursing through my bloodstream. In fact, the quickest way to make the morning haze even more unbearable is an encounter with the ever-energetic "morning person."

Whenever I encounter the dreaded morning person, I try my best to let nods and smiles hold up my end of the conversation. Around 10AM, when the coffee has worked its magic, I'll swing back by the morning person and figure out what was actually being said earlier.

C'mon, don't' judge me; you know that's how it goes down. The Bible even backs me up on this one. Proverbs 27:14 says, "If anyone loudly blesses their neighbor early in the morning, it will be taken as a curse." See, morning people? Take it down a notch. ☺

As much as I despise getting up in the morning, my children have taken it to ridiculous proportions. I've roused my son, Austin, out of bed at 2:00 in the afternoon. My oldest, Kayla, who is off at college, told me the other day she didn't get up until 4PM. What's up with that? Do all college students have a "third shift" schedule?

Catching up on sleep is one thing, but laziness as a lifestyle is sin. The Bible has clear warnings for the person who can't summon the strength to get out of bed. Proverbs 26:14 says, "As a door turns on its hinges, so a sluggard turns on his bed."

I struggle with this part of my makeup. The Christian mainstream would say that to be like Christ, we should mimic His habits as well. Mark 1:35 says, "Very early in the morning, while it was still dark, Jesus got up, left the house and went off to a solitary place, where he prayed." This would seem to indicate that this was Jesus' habit; however, the passage follows with Peter and the disciples looking everywhere for him, which might indicate that this was unexpected behavior. We see other examples of Jesus spending time with the Father well into the night, the Garden of Gethsemane being the obvious example of an all-nighter.

I certainly see the value of starting the day in the Word and getting in the right frame of mind to face the world, but sometimes I'm just not there mentally or spiritually at the crack of dawn. I'm on automatic pilot until I really wake up with the morning cup of joe. That's when I'll have a moment of devotion to start the day. My heavier time with the scripture is usually later in the day or evening when the juices are really flowing.

In my night-owl opinion, as long as you're spending time daily with the Father, the timing is not prescriptive. So, when the well-meaning Christian morning person espouses the necessity of spending time with God before the newspaper is delivered, just turn the other cheek…to the other side of the pillow.[34]

"Wake up, sleeper, rise from the dead, and Christ will shine on you." - Ephesians 5:14

Father, you deserve quantities of our time that give evidence to the importance of our relationship. You've extended an open invitation to enjoy Your presence through prayer. Help us to resist the urge to fill that crucial time with temporal pursuits.

Doughnut Bites

In 1937, Vernon Rudolph and two friends had $25 between them. With borrowed ingredients they produced the first batch of Krispy Kreme doughnuts. Bless you, Vernon Rudolph.

Lazy Tales – Git-R-Done

I may have a touch of laziness, but when I finally decide it's time to do something, you'd better get out of the way because I'm not stopping until it's done. I get that work ethic from my dad; he doesn't know when to stop either. Some switch will flip in my mind and then I'm in "Git-R-Done" mode. The progression looks a little like this:

Step One: A project is added to the list

Step Two: "I'll get right on that"

Step Three: La-Z-Boy time (planning, of course)

Step Four: Procrastination reaches critical mass

Step Five: Shift into Git-R-Done mode

Step Six: Ignore everything else in life until project is complete

Slow and steady never really worked for me. For longer projects I have more of a "hare" mentality – sprint, take a break, sprint, get distracted, sprint, sorry I dozed off, sprint to the finish line.

A perfect example would be my basement project. I decided that I wanted to explore my inner construction worker and finish my basement. When it was done, I went back and looked at the dates on my receipts. A home-improvement professional could have knocked it out in a couple of months, but from start to finish it took me four years. That 10-month break where I didn't do anything certainly didn't help. Lots of La-Z-Boy planning time mixed in there, but by the end of the project I was on a mission, and now I'm sitting in my "man cave" writing devotions. Ah, the sweet feeling of accomplishment.

The person whose life is ruled by laziness is not familiar with the Git-R-Done mode. God gave us the blessing of work because he knows that the human spirit needs a steady diet of accomplishment. Proverbs 21:25 says, "The craving of a sluggard will be the death of him, because his hands refuse to work." Hear the regret in that verse. Everyone has desires and cravings. The lazy person never achieves those goals because they won't put forth the effort it takes to make it happen.

That holds true in our spiritual life as well. Ephesians 2:10 says, "For we are God's handiwork, created in Christ Jesus to do good works, which God prepared in advance for us to do." When we receive Christ as our Savior we receive all the blessings of salvation. One of those blessings is a spiritual "honey-do" list that God prepared for us in advance. These "good works" are designed to build our spiritual muscles, draw us closer to Him, and ultimately to bring Him glory. The Holy Spirit inside us craves to be about the Father's work.

Maybe you've had periods like me where you're just not plugged into the Father's will like you should be. That's when the craving becomes the death of us. The Holy Spirit will have His way and it will either result in the death of our disobedience or the death of our fellowship with the Father. That's enough for me get out of the La-Z-Boy, shift into Git-R-Done mode, and be about the Father's business.

Father, give us the courage and strength to accomplish the tasks You've set before us. Help us to see the impact of spiritual laziness, not only in our own personal growth, but in the lives You would have us touch with Your love.

Does Different Equal Wrong?

This may come as a shock to you, but people are different. I know it's a hard concept, but let it sink in for a minute. I once heard someone say "different doesn't mean wrong," but that's a blanket statement that deserves some scrutiny.

Certainly, physical qualities that originate with birth fall into that category. Skin color, height, and physical strength are not "wrong" in any way. What about personality types? I'm an introvert by nature. I'm perfectly fine with alone time or sitting by myself at a restaurant, although I do enjoy time with family and friends. Some introverts are more extreme and go out of their way to avoid human contact. Different, but not wrong.

My oldest daughter is the opposite: she's an extrovert and needs constant human interaction. Alone time for her means she's missing out on a party somewhere. I have one friend who describes herself as an "explosivert." After hearing her reaction to something funny, you'd understand what that means. Different, but not wrong.

How about music styles? I've never been much of a country music fan, but everyone else in my family seems to enjoy it. There's a constant battle on a road trip to control the dial on the radio. For every hour they get for Taylor Swift, I get an hour for Barry Manilow. As I belt out a stirring rendition of *Mandy*, the kids usually scramble for their ear buds. Different, but not wrong.

Easy enough so far, right? Now let's get serious – college football. I was born and raised in Alabama. When someone discovers that fact about me, the next question without fail is "Auburn or Alabama?"

I'm one of the rare individuals that changed allegiance over the course of my life. I grew up in a Crimson Tide family; mom was a Bama graduate, so I naturally gravitated in that direction. When it was time to choose a college, however, Auburn was the only choice for my career path, so I was off to the enemy camp. It wasn't long before I learned the errors of my youth, and now I bleed Blue and Orange.

I enjoy cheering for my team and some light-hearted competition, but the trash talking between teams often gets out of hand. I've seen families torn apart and completely stop talking to each other because of a silly game. C'mon people – different, but not wrong.

So far the "different doesn't mean wrong" corollary is holding, but what about in the spiritual realm? I'm sure you've seen the "Coexist" bumper sticker compose of symbols from the world's major religions. If the thought behind this traveling ideology is to avoid violence because of differing beliefs, then I'm on board with that.

However, I think the underlying message in this cleverly designed word is much deeper - that all religions are equal - and with that idea I must disagree. This devotion is not the place for a full treatise of the different religions, but the basic tenets of the different faiths are diametrically opposed. In the Highlander movie franchise there was a single theme – "There can be only one." All the world religions cannot be correct. There can be only one.

Consider this - only Christianity offers:

1. A sacred text that is backed by 100% accurate prophetic revelation

2. A Savior who backed up His words with miraculous deeds

3. A Savior who is raised from the dead. Other religions revere leaders that are still in the grave

4. The testimony of changed lives (mine being one)

Jesus said in John 14:6, "I am the way and the truth and the life. No one comes to the Father except through me." This statement leaves no room for interpretation. There is only one way. The other world religions offer different ways to achieve salvation. In this case, different does mean wrong.

"Jesus does not give recipes that show the way to God as other teachers of religion do. He is himself the way." - Karl Barth

Father, You have created a world of diverse people that reflect Your innumerable characteristics. Help us to value those differences while holding firm to the truth of scripture.

The 10,000-Hour Rule

Two down, one to go. My wife and I have survived teaching two of the three kiddos to drive. Let me tell you, there are few things in life scarier than sitting in the passenger seat and answering the question, "Now, which one is the gas?" As the third child begins his training, I gave him the same sage advice that my daughters heard:

"Now listen up. Carrie Underwood made a great song, but let's get one thing clear – if you get us into trouble, it's up to you to get us out. Jesus is NOT going to take the wheel."

After that concept sinks in for a moment, I hit them with a harder-to-accept truth.

"If an animal runs in front of the car, you'll need to make a very quick decision. If you can't safely dodge or stop the car in time, (pause for effect) you may have to brace yourself and hit the animal."

You'd think I had just sanctioned the genocide of an entire race of people judging from the looks on their faces. I try to explain the difference in that scenario if it's a child instead of an animal; you swerve at all costs, even if it endangers your safety. It's all about trying to prepare them for scenarios that they may face.

Trouble seems to be around every bend in the early days of driver training. Some mailboxes were missed by inches, drivers cut off because of failure to look in the rearview mirror, pesky curbs jumping out in front of us, etc. My oldest, Kayla, was the third car involved in a bumper car scenario. Her response was expected. "I'll never drive on that road again!"

All of these near-death experiences remind me of my early driving days. Unlike the expensive driver's education courses that we are required to purchase in Georgia, we had Drivers Ed provided as a class in high school. Every day three of us would join Mr. Gilbert for a relaxing drive around the rural neighborhoods of Sylvania, AL. Relaxing, that is, unless you were driving with Ray. Ray was a guy in my class and his eyesight was, shall we say, less than 20/20 (i.e., very thick lenses). This is a sample of a typical outing with Ray at the wheel:

Mr. Gilbert: "Ray, there's a dog in the road up there."

Ray: No response, and no reduction in speed.

Mr. Gilbert: "Ray, the dog is not moving."

Ray: Cranes his head forward a little, squinting, still not slowing down. Everyone else in the car is pressing their imaginary brakes in the floorboard.

Mr. Gilbert: "RAY, STOP THE CAR!"

Ray stands on the brakes and swerves just in time to miss the dog. My friend on the driver's side got a good look at the dog as his head whizzed past the window and swore he could see tears in his eyes.

Learning to drive is like learning to do anything. At first, you're just not very good at it and it's uncomfortable, even frightening. Like most people, I was terrified of public speaking, but after countless presentations at work and teaching a Sunday School class, it's become second nature to me.

Malcolm Gladwell postulated in his book *Outliers* that a beginner would need to put in 10,000 hours of effort to become an expert in any field. I think this applies to spiritual maturity as well. Think of a person that you consider a "spiritual giant." I would wager that this person has followed the "10,000-Hour Rule" to achieve his or her level of maturity.

Consider Psalm 1:1-3, which says, "Blessed is the one who does not walk in step with the wicked or stand in the way that sinners take or sit in the company of mockers, but whose delight is in the law of the Lord, and who <u>meditates on his law day and night</u>. That person is like a tree planted by streams of water, which yields its fruit in season and whose leaf does not wither— whatever they do prospers. (emphasis mine)" A fruitful life is born out of meditating on God's word. If we do that as suggested, day and night, we'll be well on our way to 10,000 hours.

Father, we're grateful for every moment that we get to spend with You. Please use that time to train us for the challenges ahead. There are unexpected gotchas on the road of life and You are the only teacher who can teach us how to navigate them.

Let Go of the Rope

When I was around seventeen (which is how most funny stories start), I got talked into trying my hand at water-skiing. So, one fine Saturday afternoon my friends and I launched the bass boat onto the Tennessee River for some high-speed antics and daring, aquatic acrobatics. At least that was the cover story. I think I was more concerned with not looking like an idiot. But, alas, my ego was in for some rough waters that day.

After my friends demonstrated the proper technique and how "easy and fun" water skiing was, it was my turn to give it a try. I assumed the position – in the water, skis pointed up, knees slightly bent, and a firm grasp on the rope handle. I gave the driver a hearty "GO!" and he gunned it.

I got up out of the water on my first try, but it didn't last long. The natural tendency the first time you ski is to pull the rope toward you. This makes your feet fly out from under you, so within about two seconds I wiped out.

After a few failed attempts, I finally forced myself to keep my arms locked and voila! – I'm skiing. Oh yeah, I'm skiing, and I'm feeling pretty good about myself. "This skiing stuff is easy," I'm thinking, until my friend decided to turn the boat and I'm introduced to the concept of a wake.

When I hit the wake, my right foot came almost all the way out of the ski. I was literally dragging my right ski down the Tennessee River with my big toe. I continued to perform my modified slalom technique while my friends were busting a gut with laughter. After a while, my left leg eventually gave out and I took a header into the river.

That would have been the end of the story, but this was my first head-first crash and I forgot the most important tip from my thirty second training session - always let go of the rope. As I was about to learn, if you don't let go of the rope, the angle of your body drives you straight down.

Just before I start dredging the bottom of the river, I come to my senses and let go. I'm sure it was only about 3 seconds that I held on, but I still had to swim a good distance to get to the surface. After such a harrowing experience it was nice to be met with the comforting sound of hysterical laughter from my comrades.

Seems like a simple idea – just let go of the rope -- but letting go is often very difficult. There are ropes that we need to let go of in our spiritual lives as well. Maybe it's a toxic relationship that you think will eventually turn around. Maybe it's a habitual sin that we return to time and again. These are the things in life that will drive us farther and farther down into the river and separate us from fellowship with God.

Hebrews 12:1-2 says, "Therefore, since we are surrounded by such a great cloud of witnesses, let us throw off everything that hinders and <u>the sin that so easily entangles</u>. And let us run with perseverance the race marked out for us, fixing our eyes on Jesus, the pioneer and perfecter of faith."

Sin entangles us and, just like that ski rope, drags us down. But that verse also talks about a "great cloud of witnesses." These are people that God has graciously placed in our lives to help when we need to let go of the rope of sin. They can point you to helpful verses and pray with you as you learn how to let go.

Father, I pray that we'll be honest with ourselves and the areas that we struggle with. Please give us the strength to let those things go. Help us to seek out a brother or sister in Christ and ask them to pray for us. Thank You for the assurance that no matter how far we sink, You're always there to pull us up to the surface and forgive us when we turn back to You.

I've Fallen and I Can't Get Up

This next story also took place when I was seventeen. Ah yes, seventeen, the year that parents hope their kids simply survive doing stupid things. I was no exception.

The summer of my seventeenth year I worked as a waiter at Pizza Hut. It was not one of my favorite gigs, I must say. For example, on one occasion I approached a table where a couple was seated. The husband was a big, burly guy. I started with my usual opening spiel.

"Hi, my name is Lane and I'll be your waiter."

This guy looked up at me, rolled his eyes, and said, "Boy, why don't you get yourself a man's job...like driving a truck?" How does one respond to that? I got to serve quite a few interesting characters that summer.

One of the less enjoyable parts of the Pizza Hut job were nights I was scheduled to close. That meant after locking the doors at midnight, we put on our Mr. Clean aprons and cleaned the place from top to bottom.

I was mopping the floor one fateful evening and 17-year-old bad judgment made an appearance. The floors were ceramic tile and became very slick when wet. Couple that with rubber-soled shoes and you've got a 17-year-old's playground. With a running go I could slide a good 25 feet.

On my last attempt to set a world record in the ceramic-tile-sliding category, something went wrong. I remember my feet leaving the ground and trying to turn my body so I could catch myself with my hands. Unfortunately, my forehead beat my hands to the ground. The next thing I remember, I was looking up at my mom as the paramedics loaded me into the ambulance.

My parents lived 20 minutes away, so I'd been unconscious for a half hour. I turned out to be fine except for a whopper of a headache. Looking back, I realize it wasn't my sliding technique that was the problem; I just needed to fall better.

I learned that lesson again a few years ago. Back in the day, I don't know, maybe around age seventeen, I was pretty good at roller skating. Speed was the name of the game back then and I would race around the rink at blazing speeds. This would sometimes end in spectacular wipeouts, but at age seventeen I would just pop back up and keep going.

As my kids reached the skating years, I was eager to help them learn. It didn't take long for me to realize that although I was still a pretty good skater, I didn't fall nearly as well. After a couple of wipeouts and unplanned splits, I was calling in my wife to tag me out.

The key in both of those examples was developing the skill of falling. That may sound odd, but ask any athlete and they will tell you – getting knocked down is inevitable; learning to fall correctly is the key to minimizing injury.

There's a spiritual application there too – life is a contact sport and we're going to get knocked down. How do we learn to minimize injury? Psalm 37:23-24 says, "The Lord makes firm the steps of the one who delights in him; though he may stumble, he will not fall, for the Lord upholds him with his hand."

Have you ever stumbled and had the person nearby keep you from taking a nasty fall? The same is true of our walk with the Lord. If we "delight in Him" then we are walking closely beside Him; when the trials of life make us stumble, we can grab His hand so that he can keep us from going down.

But what if you've already taken a tumble? You've said or done something that has damaged your relationship with family, a friend, or the Lord. You feel like you've fallen so far away from

Him that there's just no way to fix it. Take heart; there is no place so far from the Lord that he will not graciously pick you up.

Psalm 40:1-2 says, "I waited patiently for the Lord; he turned to me and heard my cry. He lifted me out of the slimy pit, out of the mud and mire; he set my feet on a rock and gave me a firm place to stand." A slimy pit - what a great word picture. I've been to that slimy pit; when I felt like I had so disappointed my Lord that He would never want to be around me again. Praise God that falling is not the end. If we walk closely with Him he can keep us from falling, but when we do He promises to pick us up.

Learning to minimize the damage when we fall is an important spiritual skill. Let's recap:

1. Walk closely with Christ and He will prevent a stumble from turning into a major fall

2. When we do fall, reach up for the Lord. He will pull you up and put you back on a firm footing.

3. Continue your journey with the Lord. Only by spending time with Him do we learn how avoid and minimize the damage of a fall.

Father, we are a fragile creation, physically, and, all too often, spiritually. The stumbles we experience are sometimes unforeseen, but sometimes because of our own poor choices. Thank You for Your grace and faithfulness to pick us up when we fall.

Selective Deafness

Most people fall into one of two categories – cat person or dog person. I had both growing up, so I was on the fence when it came to a favorite; that is, until we got a cat named Beethoven.

Beethoven was a white cat with blue eyes. After we adopted him we learned that white cats with blue eyes are usually deaf…and he was…deaf as a doornail. That's where the name Beethoven came from; the composer was also deaf. There's some useful trivia to impress your friends with at the next Trivial Pursuit party.

Imagine the frustration of a pet that you can't discipline by yelling at them. Granted, cats don't listen much anyway, but a loud noise will usually make them stop scratching the couch. To get Beethoven's attention you had to walk over and get in his face or throw something at him. It was very frustrating. We eventually found a spray bottle that had excellent distance, so I could soak him from across the room from my La-Z-Boy.

The deafness probably explains why he just seemed to get into everything. One day we came home to find him swinging in the chandelier. We're still not sure how he got up there. That was one crazy cat.

My wife would contend that I'm a lot like Beethoven at times. Yes, I suffer from a malady known as Selective Deafness. I usually have an SD attack if one of the following circumstances occurs:

1. There are two minutes left in the game and my team is driving for the win

2. The murderer is about to be revealed

3. The punch line is being delivered

There are other flare ups, but most SD attacks are related somehow to the television. I'm sure I'm not the only husband afflicted with this disease. Thankfully, the Lord saw that this was a constant source of conflict and created the greatest marital aid of the 21st century – the DVR. Now I'm able to pause the TV and give my wife the full attention she deserves without missing the game winning play. Thank you Lord!

I wonder if the Lord has similar frustration when we are guilty of another kind of SD – Spiritual Deafness? God loves us and wants to bless us, so why is it so hard for Him to get our attention? I'm sure some would say busyness is a culprit, but I think there's a deeper issue – we don't want to hear from God because then we'd have to choose whether or not to obey Him.

Hebrews 4:7 says, "Today, if you hear his voice, do not harden your hearts." I think that's the scenario we'd like to avoid. Sometimes I think we believe that if we walk closely enough to hear His voice, He may ask us to do something that we're not prepared to do. We don't want to be disobedient, so we just avoid hearing from Him altogether.

Consider this promise from John 10:27-28 which says, "My sheep listen to my voice; I know them, and they follow me. I give them eternal life, and they shall never perish; no one will snatch them out of my hand." That should bring a lot of comfort to those that hear his voice; however, the flipside is true as well. John 8:47 says "Whoever belongs to God hears what God says. The reason you do not hear is that you do not belong to God." That can be tough to hear, but sometimes a little self-examination is just what we need.

Let me encourage you to listen to His voice – through prayer, the scriptures, or a stirring in your spirit. The Lord won't ask of you more than you can bear, but learning to hear and obey Him is part of the blessing of being His child. Plus, if you find yourself stuck in a chandelier, He's there to help you down.

Father, give us courage to listen to Your voice and obey. Show us that listening to friends, family and even pastors is not enough; we need to hear directly from You. Make us familiar with Your voice. Make us responsive to Your call. Give us an unquenchable desire to follow You.

Doughnut Bites

The "Doughnut Dollies" doled out doughnuts in WWI and WWII. In their honor, the Salvation army started celebrating National Doughnut Day the first Friday in June. It's been a national holiday since 1982.

Knowledge is Power

At a recent family gathering we were discussing what kind of careers our children might be interested in. One of my children rattled off a couple of options to which my brother replied, "Nah, you don't want to do that. You want to learn to do something that very few people know how to do. That's where the money is."

There's some truth in that: our culture places a high value on unique knowledge and skills, and people who master that knowledge are rewarded handsomely. You've heard the saying, "It's not rocket science." People say that because they know that rocket science is hard and few people master it. The ones that do aren't hurting for a little coin.

The Lord places a great deal of value on knowledge as well. Consider these verses:

> Gold there is, and rubies in abundance, but lips that speak knowledge are a <u>rare jewel</u>. – Prov. 20:15

> Choose my instruction instead of <u>silver</u>, knowledge rather than choice <u>gold</u>, for wisdom is more precious than <u>rubies</u>, and nothing you desire can compare with her. – Prov. 8:10-11

> My goal is that they may be encouraged in heart and united in love, so that they may have the <u>full riches of complete understanding</u>, in order that they may know the mystery of God, namely, Christ, in whom are hidden all the <u>treasures of wisdom and knowledge</u>. – Col. 2:2-3

The scriptures equate knowledge with the things that humans consider of greatest material value – jewels, silver, gold and treasure. Knowledge of God is greater than all these things. Consider this – what is the most "valuable" thing that we receive from salvation? I would submit that eternal life as opposed to eternal death is a priceless gift that we receive when we come to Christ. Here's the kicker – what is eternal life? John 17:3 spells it out clearly:

> "Now this is eternal life: that they know you, the only true God, and Jesus Christ, whom you have sent."

Eternal life = knowledge of God. It's more than just knowing biblical facts; it's a personal, intimate, relational knowledge of our Heavenly Father that is more valuable than any earthly treasure.

You'd think something this valuable would be hard to find or difficult to obtain, but it's just the opposite. The Lord has made the truth of who He is available to any who will receive it. No treasure maps, no secret clues: all we have to do is open the Bible and bask in the treasure trove of knowledge. It's not rocket science…it's more valuable than that.

Father, thank you for the treasure of knowing You. Give us a passion to know You that eclipses all other pursuits.

Politics Make Strange Bedfellows

A friend of ours is a city councilman running for reelection. He's a fine Christian man trying to make a difference in the public arena. Even though we live in an adjacent city, my wife and I would love to see him succeed so we're both making donations to his campaign.

My wife is donating her time as his campaign manager and I'm donating…well…my time with my wife; he'll be seeing a lot more of her until the election than I will. They're both trustworthy, so I won't have to worry about that "strange bedfellows" stuff.

This whole process started me thinking. Why would the average citizen give up their time and money to see someone else get elected to office? I think there are three primary reasons:

1. Believing they are who they say they are (honest, trustworthy, etc.) and will do what they say they will do.

2. Believing the (city, state, country) will be a better place with them in office.

3. Believing your own condition will be improved by the policies they implement.

Of course, it doesn't always work out that way. Humans are weak and susceptible to the corruption that so often accompanies politics. We place a certain amount of faith in humans and most will let us down eventually.

Now consider Christ. Why do people place their trust in Christ? Why do His followers donate their time and money to tell others about Him? I think some of the reasons are the same:

1. You believe He is who He says He is (Savior, Lord of Lords, God incarnate, etc.) and will do what He says He will do (reconcile us to the Father and give us eternal life).

2. You believe the (city, state, country) will be a better place if people turn to Him (school shootings will decrease, children will have stable homes with Him at the center, and the world will be transformed by His love).

3. You believe your own condition will be improved by following Him.

So, why is it so much easier to get people fired up about the political candidate of their choice? Do these fallible men and women deserve more faith than the Savior who died for us?

Is it because we can see and hear the candidates on the stump? Can we not see the visible effects of Christ in people's lives and our own lives? Can we not see the world's downward spiral as a result of not following Him?

Let's turn it around. Let's go to rallies for Christ. Let's shake hands and kiss babies as we tell them about His love. Let's wear His character like a campaign sticker. Let's get out the vote for Christ. Tell people about his "platform" of love, forgiveness and sacrifice. Election Day is coming when the ballots will be cast. He's going to win! Let's treat the Great Commission like a Great Campaign to tell people about the Lord.

Father, thank You for sending Your Son to be our Savior. Jesus is the name above all names and there is no other name under heaven given to mankind by which we must be saved.[35] There are no other suitable candidates. Give us a passion to donate our lives to communicating the Gospel.

Car Wash of Fear

As a parent, part of my job is to calm the fears of my children. The world can be very scary for kids as they encounter places and situations that are new to them. Historically, my wife and I have done a good job protecting them and calming their fears, but there have been a few unfortunate times when we totally misread a situation.

For example, who would have thought a car wash would result in hysterical screaming from my two young daughters in the back seat? Sonya had to unbuckle and crawl in the back to calm them down until the rinse cycle was complete.

On another occasion we went tubing on a fairly lazy river with a few other families. My kids are good swimmers and they had enough life jackets to keep the Titanic afloat, but it wasn't fear of water that was the problem. My middle daughter, Cassidy, was totally freaking out about the large boulders that we were floating lazily over. Again, we had to pull her close and reassure her that the rocks were not a concern.

You'd think we would be a bit more cautious, but we had another #fail moment when we took the girls to Disney World. Sonya and I were certain that they were ready for Space Mountain (I'm sure you can see where this is headed, but don't get ahead of me). We remembered that it was a speedy ride, but we must have blocked out the darkness and that loud red tube at the end.

We learned that day that the height requirement shouldn't be the sole determining factor for a child getting on a ride. They had a good old-fashioned come-apart on that roller coaster. We felt like the worst parents ever. I won't tell you about Big Thunder Mountain Railroad later in the day lest I confirm that assertion.

Sure, some childhood fears are unfounded, but we face legitimate fears all too often. Even those with great faith are not immune. Take King David, for example. Psalm 55:4-5 says, "My heart is in anguish within me; the terrors of death have fallen on me. Fear and trembling have beset me; horror has overwhelmed me."

Maybe you've experienced that level of fear as well. When those situations arise, we need to continue to listen to the "man after God's own heart." Continuing in verses 16-18 of chapter 55, David says "As for me, I call to God, and the Lord saves me. Evening, morning and noon I cry out in distress, and he hears my voice. He rescues me unharmed from the battle waged against me, even though many oppose me."

Notice that the Lord doesn't stop the battle; it keeps raging around David, but the Lord preserves him through it. He'll do the same for us. Our gracious Father invites us in 1 Peter 5:7 to "cast all our anxieties on him because he cares for you." He will meet us in our fear and pull us under his sheltering wing. I'm sure He'd even join you in the back seat if your parents left you with an unnatural fear of car washes.

Father, we live in a world that can shake us to the core. War, disease, and those that want to do us harm are legitimate concerns. Father, give us a calming dose of Your Spirit to ensure us that You are greater than those against us. You are greater than our greatest fear.

Preparing for Doomsday

Dictionary.com and Webster's Dictionary need to keep up with the times a little better. When I look up the word *prepping,* they talk about "getting ready" or "going to a prep school." The Urban Dictionary has it right – "to store items such as food, water and ammo in preparation for a disaster of any type such as a hurricane, tornado, or economic collapse."

My first exposure to prepping was in conjunction with Y2K. The Y2K doomsday pundits made a compelling argument, but turned out to be very wrong. I think I still have some dehydrated water in the basement (just add water).

These days, prepping has found new life. Google has an interesting graph[36] of the occurrence of the word "prepping" in published books. The chart shows an exponential increase in the last few years.

Why? I think it's because we live in a world that is constantly inundated with crises – terrorism, a new disease that will wipe us out, a dysfunctional government - you name it, there's no end to potential threats to our security. When people are confronted with uncertainty, they tend to circle the wagons, or in the case of the extreme preppers, build a bomb shelter in Wyoming.

We want to ensure our families' safety and future, right? The Bible agrees, with many verses about the wisdom of planning ahead:

- *"Go to the ant, you sluggard; consider its ways and be wise! It has no commander, no overseer or ruler, yet it stores its provisions in summer and gathers its food at harvest."* – Proverbs 6:6-8

- *"Wise people think before they act; fools don't – and even brag about their foolishness."* – Proverbs 13:16 NLT

However, our race to accumulate a lifetime supply of toilet paper must be balanced against our standing orders to make disciples.[37] The Great Commission is not suspended when times get tough. You may need to take some action to circle the wagons, but the Lord will always give us opportunities to share His love with a dying world.

Father, we live in stressful times. We can see realistic scenarios that could impact our safety. Remind us that Christ left the safety of Heaven to share the Father's love with us. We are called to do the same.

Burn, Baby, Burn

There are some words in the English language that *sound* just like their meaning. Take the word "chores," for instance. Say it out loud – "chores." See, you frowned a little and sighed, didn't you?

We get introduced to this lovely word early in life, usually when our parents get tired of cleaning up our mess and want some well-deserved help. Through the discipline of learning to do chores we learn responsibility, the value of cleanliness, and blah, blah, blah. It's no use; I can't even put a positive spin on it. Chores are of the devil.

Growing up with two brothers, the arguments over chores were nonstop.

"Why do I have to unload the dishwasher? You never make Jay unload the dishwasher!"

It probably had something to do with Jay being four years old and handling knives, but so what! It still wasn't fair. However, as we got older, there was one chore that we actually fought over – burning the garbage.

Before the advent of garbage service, we country folk had to dispose of our trash in different ways. Leftovers were easy; just dump them in the backyard and the nearest neighborhood dog would wander by in a matter of minutes. For larger items, a trip to the dump was the solution, but for run-of-the-mill trash, most people had a 50-gallon drum to set it ablaze.

Since there's a budding pyromaniac inside most teenage boys, this was great fun. The only tricky part was using paper matchbooks. A wooden match was a rare treat, so we were stuck trying to develop our inner arsonist with paper matches.

Lighting a paper match and still walking away with a thumbprint does not come naturally. But that didn't deter us from our desired to burn everything we could get our hands on. Mom would have to stop us from taking out trash bags containing only an empty Little Debbies box in it (mmm, Swiss Cake Rolls, but I digress).

When we did get a full bag, it was awesome to watch it all go up in flames. Pop bottles would explode and then hiss as the plastic melted. Leftover food would release various odors as it was consumed by flames. We would add anything lying around to keep the fun going as long as possible. I feel sorry for today's kids who never learn the simple joys of burning stuff.

Then there was the day that I found one of my old toys about to be incinerated. I didn't care that Stretch Armstrong was stretched one too many times and leaking whatever that inner goo was, I had to save him. So, I reach into the flames and plucked him from certain death. How could mom think that Stretch was no longer valuable?

There are a lot of items I still find valuable that I would not want to see go up in flames. However, all our "stuff" will be tested with fire one day. 1 Corinthians 3:11-15 says, "For no one can lay any foundation other than the one already laid, which is Jesus Christ. If anyone builds on this foundation using gold, silver, costly stones, wood, hay or straw, their work will be shown for what it is, because the Day will bring it to light. It will be <u>revealed with fire</u>, and the <u>fire will test the quality of each person's work</u>. If what has been built survives, the builder will receive a reward. If

it is burned up, the builder will suffer loss but yet will be saved—
even though only as one escaping through the flames."

Christ is the foundation. What are you building on that
foundation? Disciples, relationships, and acts of service are
examples of building materials that will endure the fires of
judgment. Houses, cars, 401K, and Stretch Armstongs will not.

I don't know about you, but when I get to Heaven I'd like to be
able to present my Lord with a structure that will stand up under
His righteous scrutiny. It would be a shame for all my efforts to
end up burning in Heaven's 50-gallon garbage drum.

*Father, You've blessed us with a foundation of Christ and given us
opportunities to build something to bring You glory. Help us stay
focused on the eternal and not put all our energy into temporal "stuff."*

Salvation by Extension Cord

On August 29, 2005, Hurricane Katrina knocked the breath out of New Orleans. I had a chance to go down as part of a cleanup team a few weeks after the initial blow. Power had just been restored, but people were still dazed.

Words are insufficient to communicate the devastation I witnessed. Houses near the shoreline were simply bare lots; the remains of the actual structure several hundred yards further inland. What used to be concrete steps leading to a front door now led to empty air. Entire sections of concrete bridges were missing. Steeples reclined in the front yards of churches instead of their lofty perches.

The houses that did survive were ravaged by flood damage. We did mud-outs on three houses. Our job was to go in and remove everything in the house below the flood line – all the way to the studs.

The flood line in the first house was clearly evident at about three feet. Everything below that was contaminated by the flood waters and had to go. The flood line at the second house could be seen in the vaulted ceilings, about 12 feet up. There was no flood line in the third house. It was completely submerged.

However, the property damage paled in comparison to the human tragedy. Every cleanup team had a chaplain as a team member to minister to the residents as we performed the cleanup. I found some family photos at one house and took them out to the homeowner. Tears erupted; emotions were always close to the

surface and with every destroyed heirloom, the wound was reopened. She took the photos, carefully removed them from the frames, and laid them in the sun to dry.

We sat in a Red Cross tent for lunch one day and I met a man with quite a story to tell. When the storm hit he was cut off from his home by the flood waters. As the water continued to rise he was forced to climb to the very top of a tree. He spent several hours with no sign of rescue and was beginning to succumb to fatigue and cold. As hope faded, he began to pray for a miracle. I'll never forget what he said next, with a catch in his voice.

"Then the Lord sent me an extension cord."

I still tear up when I think about it. An extension cord floated to him and with his last ounce of energy he tied himself to the trunk of the tree. He was able to hang there until help arrived. He found salvation in an extension cord.

Do you sometimes feel like you're hanging on with the last ounce of your energy? The enemy can come at us with hurricane-force winds; so much so that we may be tempted to give in to his destructive power. Take heart, brother or sister, because there is hope in Christ.

When we lose the strength to carry on, he'll be our extension cord. We can tie on to Him and rely on His strength until the storm passes. Psalm 107:29 says, "Then they cried out to the Lord in their trouble, and he brought them out of their distress. He stilled the storm to a whisper; the waves of the sea were hushed." New Orleans got its breath back when it was knocked out. You will too.

Father, the storms of life are ferocious at times. We praise You because You are the one who calms the storm. Be our strength in the absence of our own.

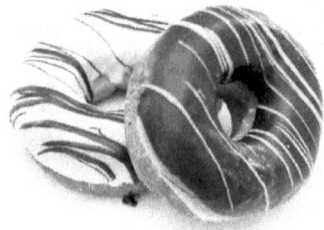

An Angel Named Thunder

"Hey brother, can you spare some change?"

I work in downtown Atlanta, so I hear this request a couple of times a week. Some of the downtrodden have better marketing plans than others, including signs with different variations of the standard buzz words - "Hungry, homeless, God bless." I once saw a man with a sign that read "I need beer." I guess he thought honesty was the best policy.

As Christ-followers, this can present a conundrum. On one hand, we are called to minister to the poor. Consider these clear mandates from scripture:

> "Give to the one who asks you, and do not turn away from the one who wants to borrow from you." Matthew 5:42

> "For I was hungry and you gave me something to eat, I was thirsty and you gave me something to drink, I was a stranger and you invited me in, I needed clothes and you clothed me, I was sick and you looked after me, I was in prison and you came to visit me." Matthew 25:35-36

> "Whoever is kind to the poor lends to the Lord, and he will reward them for what they have done." Proverbs 19:17

So, according to these verses, we should walk around with an open wallet and toss dollars out like candy at a Christmas parade, right? But what about the following scripture?

"For even when we were with you, we gave you this rule: 'The one who is unwilling to work shall not eat.' We hear that some among you are idle and disruptive. They are not busy; they are busybodies. Such people we command and urge in the Lord Jesus Christ to settle down and earn the food they eat." 2 Thessalonians 3:10-12

We know the score, right? Some people who are "down on their luck" have chosen this lifestyle. There are people, perfectly capable of working, who choose to be professional beggars, content to live off the generosity of others. But I fear we overuse Paul's warning as an excuse to turn a blind eye to the daily needs we encounter.

It's true; there must be some wisdom in our giving. If we met every empty hand with a wad of cash, we'd quickly find ourselves in a similar situation. However, a quick survey of scripture will reveal a much heavier weighting for verses encouraging generosity. Our Savior is the prototype for giving, eventually giving his very life for our salvation.

So, what is the conscientious Christian to do? Ultimately, I think the answer is found in a daily, personal walk with Christ. If we are in the Word and faithful in prayer, we will be able to discern His leading in these situations. The Holy Spirit will speak and guide us to ministry opportunities. I've sensed a clear leading on several occasions. On one day in particular I was blessed to meet an angel named Thunder.

Let me paint the scene – the interstate off-ramp that I use at the end of my daily commute is a common hangout for those looking for help from tired commuters. To be honest, I don't typically feel led to obstruct traffic while I scramble for a donation, but on one occasion I received a strong urging to help.

The person standing on the corner had a different look to him. Young, tall, strong – he didn't fit the typical stereotype. His sign was simple" "Traveling. Assistance appreciated. God Bless." I had already made the turn off the interstate before the Holy Spirit got my attention.

"Help him."

I've missed opportunities in the past; I wasn't going to miss this one. I wanted to be responsible so I decided to stop at the grocery store and buy some items. I jumped back on the freeway and re-exited, but this time I pulled over and introduced myself.

As I approached, I got a better look at my "mission project" and started to second-guess myself. He was at least 6'4" with long blond hair spilling out from beneath a cowboy hat. Add some boots, various tattoos and a belt buckle the size of Texas and you start to get the picture. Oh well, no turning back now.

"Hi, I'm Lane."

"Thunder," he boomed with a smile and an outstretched hand.

At first I didn't know if he was telling me his name or if I'd stumbled upon a Norse god who was calling down thunder from heaven. Assuming this wasn't Thor's long lost brother, I continued.

We exchanged some pleasantries and I learned that Thunder was a traveler, but more than that he was a missionary. When I offered him the bags of groceries I purchased, he graciously accepted. He said that when people gave him more than he could travel with (I went a little overboard), he shared the excess with local shelters.

I already felt small compared to his physical presence, but I was starting to shrink spiritually as well as he recounted the ways he's been able to help other brothers and sisters in need. Then he really turned the tables on me and pulled out his Bible to share some verses with me.

Wait a minute! Who is ministering to whom here?

By the end of our encounter, I was humbled. I had experienced a spiritual peal of Thunder. I don't know if I've ever unknowingly entertained an angel,[38] but Thunder would be a great candidate.

Father, give us Your heart for giving. Make us sensitive to the needs around us and give us courage to get involved in uncomfortable situations. Show us the great paradox that giving is a blessing to both the giver and recipient.

End Notes

[1] This and following doughnut facts come from Smithsonian.com - http://www.smithsonianmag.com/history-archaeology/object_mar98.html

[2] Genesis 2:4-15

[3] Romans 5:17-19

[4] http://www.extremetech.com/extreme/134672-harvard-cracks-dna-storage-crams-700-terabytes-of-data-into-a-single-gram

[5] Matthew 10:30

[6] http://www.nasa.gov/audience/foreducators/5-8/features/F_How_Big_is_Our_Universe.html

[7] http://curiosity.discovery.com/question/smallest-particles

[8] Acts 1:8

[9] http://www.atomicarchive.com/Effects/effects3.shtml

[10] Isaiah 52:14

[11] Matthew 27:52-53

[12] Isaiah 64:6

[13] John 15:4-5

[14] http://library.timelesstruths.org/music/There_Is_Power_in_the_Blood/

[15] If you know what "defenestrated" means you have a mighty vocabulary, indeed. It means "to throw something out a window."

[16] Name changed to protect the innocent

[17] Hebrews 5:12

[18] Matthew 7:21-23

[19] Genesis 1:28-29; 2:15

[20] CHRINO = CHRistian In Name Only

[21] Ephesians 2:8-9

[22] Ephesians 2:10

[23] Luke 4:42, Matthew 14:22, Luke 5:16

[24] http://plato.stanford.edu/entries/pascal-wager/

[25] An Aramaic word that means "the Lord is coming" or "come, O Lord."

[26] http://www.nps.gov/plants/alien/pubs/midatlantic/pumol.htm

[27] http://altmedicine.about.com/od/completeazindex/a/kudzu.htm

[28] Romans 12:2

[29] Judges 12:5-6

[30] The longest recorded name in the Bible is Mahershalalhashbaz, which appears in Isaiah 8:1. It means "quick to plunder, swift to spoil." Imagine calling him for dinner. I'll bet he was "hash" for short.

[31] http://www.health.harvard.edu/healthbeat/7-tips-for-a-safe-and-successful-strength-training-program

[32] Genesis 22:1

[33] Romans 8:31

[34] A couple of supporting thoughts came from http://chrisatwooddotcom.wordpress.com/

[35] Acts 4:12

[36] http://books.google.com/ngrams/graph?content=PREPPING%2BPrepping%2Bprepping&year_start=1800&year_end=2012&corpus=15&smoothing=7&share=

[37] Matthew 18:16-20

[38] Hebrews 13:2

www.ingramcontent.com/pod-product-compliance
Lightning Source LLC
Chambersburg PA
CBHW061727020426
42331CB00006B/1127